The Batterer

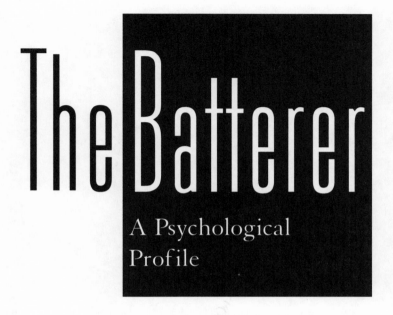

The Batterer

A Psychological Profile

DONALD G. DUTTON, Ph.D.,
WITH SUSAN K. GOLANT

BasicBooks
A Division of HarperCollinsPublishers

362.829
D981b

Designed by Elliott Beard

Library of Congress Cataloging-in-Publication Data
Dutton, Donald G., 1943–
    The batterer : a psychological profile / Donald G. Dutton with
Susan K. Golant.
        p. cm.
    Includes bibliographical references and index.
    ISBN 0–465–03387–3
    1. Abusive men—United States—Psychology.   2. Abusive men—United
States—Case studies.   3. Wife abuse—United States—Psychological aspects.
    4. Family violence—United States—Psychological aspects.
    I. Golant, Susan K.   II. Title.
    HV6626.2.D87   1995
    362.82'92—dc20   95-9556
                                                                CIP

95 96 97 98 ❖/HC 9 8 7 6 5 4 3 2 1

To Marta, for teaching me the healing power of love

Contents

Preface

TWENTY YEARS AGO, NO ONE RECOGNIZED WIFE ASSAULT AS A social problem. It was ignored in academic texts. It went unrecorded by police forces. Men were rarely arrested for beating their wives. Only shelter workers seemed aware of the magnitude of the problem. The women's movement was responsible for bringing family violence into public awareness, and in 1975 the pioneering work of sociologist Murray Straus showed us how commonplace it really is.

Psychologists, such as Lenore Walker in her classic book *The Battered Woman*, have done an excellent job of describing the psychology of the woman tangled in the complex web of abusiveness, but there has been great resistance to developing a psychology of batterers. If such a psychology were found, it was believed, it would somehow absolve the abusers' inexcusable behavior and consequently deflect efforts at sociopolitical change to diminish wife assault.

What few attempts there were to study batterers often seemed piecemeal: data disconnected from theory or vice versa. One researcher would study men's attitudes, another alcohol use, a third exposure to violence as a child. Often it seemed as though these scientists didn't read one another's work and therefore couldn't build a cumulative base of knowledge. At other times, it seemed that researchers had little clinical understanding of batterers while clinicians—those in the trenches working with abusers—seemed to ignore the latest research findings. In this book, I have sought to develop a coherent theory that relates these disparate findings and reconciles clinical experience with research studies.

It has been a long road. I began working with assaultive men in 1978, both as a clinician and as a researcher. As I conducted treatment groups for batterers, I began to wonder: How are abusive men different from other men? What had made them that way? To answer these questions I read through the literature of the sociology, psychology, and psychiatry of violence and of intimate relationships, looking for threads of understanding. At first, I thought of all batterers as a single group. Later, I began to recognize distinctions in the psychology and behavior of different types of wife assaulters.

I became particularly interested in one type, the so-called cyclical batterers, because I felt they were the most dangerous and the least understood. Their harmfulness stemmed from the serial and private nature of their violence. It was repetitive and transcended women and relationships. These men were abusive regardless of who their partner was or what she did. Moreover, they appeared to have two personalities, one at home with their partners and another in public—and even in private they seemed to undergo changes, alternately acting abusive and contrite.

The private nature of the cyclical batterers' violence also contributed to our lack of understanding. Conventional theories in psychology had passed over these men. Because their violence was hidden, they had avoided scrutiny.

Even their wives' descriptions of them in Lenore Walker's book did little to promote their further study. The politics of research still directed the search toward the cultural shaping of all men rather than to the impact of one's unique life experience on individual rage.

This book is an effort to look at batterers from a new, more psychological perspective. Rather than focus on battering as an isolated behavior, I view it as the product of an entire personality constellation. Assaultiveness exists, I believe, to maintain this personality. The acting out of abuse serves a necessary function—the abuser needs it to maintain his sense of feeling whole. And, as we shall see, this personality has its origins in early development, in the vagaries of early attachment and a father's shaming and violent behavior.

Abusiveness is not, however, just a copied behavior but rather a learned means of self-maintenance. The abusive man is addicted to brutality to keep his shaky self-concept intact. The only time he feels powerful and whole is when he is engaged in violence.

The treatment of abusiveness must consider these issues. Work on emotions stemming from the family of origin is essential. I describe treatment in this book and outline the results of the longest study ever conducted on its effectiveness—an eleven-year follow-up of treated men. I have developed a novel perspective on treatment, one that views it as a five-stage spiral process toward recovery.

The cases in this book are drawn from my therapy files. However, each case is a composite of more than one client and all names are fictitious. These composites are necessary to give voice to the themes described in therapy. It is an arduous process to find the inner voice of abusive men. The lifelong silencing of that voice contributes to the acting out of rage in place of grief or longing. The origins of that grief or longing are very early in the childhood development of the man who will be an abusive adult.

I have built this psychological model of the batterer from a large and laboriously extracted data base, carefully sifting the response patterns of abusive men and matching the resulting nuggets with the reports of their female partners.

We are about to take a trip into the mind of the abuser. It's a place of anguish and self-loathing. A place that, to be healed, must first be opened to the air.

Acknowledgments

THIS BOOK IS THE RESULT OF A TWENTY-YEAR EFFORT TO STUDY and treat abusive men. Several people have contributed to my effort and I would like to acknowledge them.

First, I am grateful to my two cotherapists in the Assaultive Husbands Program, Dale Trimble and Jim Browning, for their generosity in sharing treatment ideas and support. They were especially responsive to my queries for data collection with the clients. Other therapists in a less research-friendly environment might have been less receptive.

I am also deeply indebted to Anne Ganley, who remains the architect of treatment groups for batterers. I remember her workshops as especially rich in ideas and insights about the psychology of abusive men. I'd like to express my appreciation to Susan Painter for influencing the developmental aspects of my search for explanations; to Steve Hart for sharpening my understanding of psychopathology and teaching me how to assess it; to Linda Graham for cutting through intractable bureaucracy to facilitate research funding (and for listening to my rants about bureaucrats!); to Barbara McGregor for eight years of intellectual and logistical assistance; to Angela Browne for her critical insights and general contributions to the problem of family violence; to Murray Straus for opening the Pandora's box; and to Paul Mones for years of intellectual challenge and support.

My thanks go to my graduate students and the people who make my research lab a daily source of intellectual stimulation: Andrew Starzomski, Cynthia van Ginkel, Monica Landolt, Catherine Learmonth, Ardis Krueger.

I am also grateful to those whom I have never met but who have influenced my thinking greatly: Bessel van der Kolk, Theodore Millon, John Gunderson, John Bowlby, Margaret Mahler, Melanie Klein.

Susan Golant took my tortuous academic prose and opened it up for all to see. Jo Ann Miller was an enormously thoughtful and assiduous editor.

I'm also grateful to those men and their partners who had the courage to change and to share their fears and experiences with me.

Finally, my deepest gratitude to my wife, Marta, for being a woman of such security and independence that she could tolerate my long hours of unavailability while I banged away at my word processor.

PART I

What Is a Batterer?

1 Drowning in a Red Tide

IN FEBRUARY 1995, A HORRIFIED NATION WATCHED AND listened as Denise Brown, Nicole Simpson's sister, testified about a violent incident in the Simpson household. "Pictures started flying off the walls; clothes started flying down the stairs," she said, weeping. "He grabbed Nicole and told her to get out of the house. He picked her up and threw her out of the house. She ended up falling on her elbows and her butt."

And we asked ourselves once again, how is it possible for this beloved sports and television star, O. J. Simpson, to be so different in public and in private?

To his adoring fans, O. J. was a superhero, a legend—handsome, affable, rich, powerful—one of the greatest running backs in football history. One sponsor had him, in his superhero role, jumping airport obstacles to get to his rented car on time. He was Monday Night Football's color commentator. He acted in movies. O. J. was such a celebrity that his initials were enough for everyone to know the rest. The rest, that is, of the public image.

When Simpson was charged with killing his ex-wife and her friend, Ron Goldman, in 1994, another, darker side emerged.

Suddenly we all learned that our superhero was a wife batterer. The media played Nicole Brown Simpson's frantic 911 call to the LAPD. She was pleading for help, with O. J. ranting and cursing and breaking down the door in the background. The public was shocked. How could someone so genial, so successful, be so cruel at home?

I had never met O. J. Simpson when I was asked to testify as an expert witness on wife assault on behalf of the prosecution. I had never interviewed him for the treatment groups I run for battering men. But I had seen many others like him.

I had never met Ike Turner, either. I remember only the R&B he and Tina made in the early 1960s and their glittering Ike and Tina Turner Revues. Nevertheless, I feel that I know him too, at least as he was portrayed in the movie *What's Love Got to Do with It*. The film was about Tina's "development" as an entertainer under Ike's tutelage. It was also about her escape from his abuse and tyrannical outbursts.

In the film, Ike is portrayed as easygoing and playful with his male friends but brutal with Tina. He undermines her confidence, insults her abilities, and dominates her at every turn. Intermittently, he explodes in tirades of abuse—punching, slapping, insulting, and even raping her. He seems to be her mentor, pimp, and tormenter all in one.

After the film's release, the men in my therapy groups, men who had been convicted in court of wife assault, watched *What's Love Got to Do with It*. They thought Ike was a pretty bad guy, a lot more abusive than they had ever been. If Ike had seen a movie of their lives, he no doubt would have had the same opinion of them. I understand he was upset by the portrayal of him in the film.

We all hold stereotypes of an abusive male. He's something like Stanley Kowalski: crude, uneducated, "a pig." I was not immune to these notions either. When I first began running treatment groups for wife abusers, my initial reaction to the court-referred participants was surprise at how "normal" they seemed. They weren't all madmen or twitchy neurotics. They weren't all macho misogynists either. In fact, they seemed, on the surface, no different from the men I had passed on the street on the way to the group.

We somehow expect that hurtful people will look the part. They're not one of us—and especially not one of our heroes. So when the newspaper reports that, for example, Peter Martins, the ballet master of the New York City Ballet and former principal dancer of the Royal Danish Ballet, was briefly charged with assaulting his wife (the charge was dropped), we are startled.[1] When we hear testimony about O. J. Simpson denigrating his wife, and we become privy to the photos of her bruised and battered face, we are confused and jolted. This is not the star we know and love. This is not supposed to happen.

Indeed, as the preliminary court hearing for O. J. was aired live on all major networks, people gathered outside the courtroom, selling T-shirts that read "Pray for O. J." and O. J.'s football buddies swore their loyalty saying that he couldn't possibly have been the killer.[2]

Despite our beliefs to the contrary, however, the California prosecutors who aired the LAPD tapes punctured a great myth: that men who are violent at home have nasty public personalities. When it comes to abuse in intimate relationships, our private theories fall apart. We just can't tell the perpetrators by looking at them. And we can't understand how men who seem to "have it all together" on the outside can be abusive at home. We can't comprehend why they seem so vulnerable to the loss of a wife they themselves have driven away. Or how that vulnerability turns into a rage to destroy her.

I once interviewed a man who had killed his wife and his two children and then turned the gun on himself. It misfired. I asked him if he could explain what he had done. All he said was, "If I couldn't have them, I didn't want no one else to have them." To some, this implies that his family had become mere objects to this man rather than people. To me, it suggests that they were essential possessions: property that had to be controlled and maintained, the way a junkie would keep his drug supply.

■ The Sea of Love, The Sea of Rage

Robert was referred to one of my wife assault treatment groups while his spouse, Carol, was still hospitalized for injuries sustained as a result of his having beaten her. He was, as they say, "average looking"—medium height and build, brown hair, hazel eyes. He wore blue jeans, a denim shirt, and heavy work boots. A deep-sea diver by profession, he was in his early twenties.

In group that first night, Robert looked tense. Repeatedly clenching and unclenching his fists, he rocked back and forth in his chair while staring at the floor as if he were trying to burn a hole in it. He avoided all eye contact and seemed to be on the verge of tears whenever he was asked a question. Indeed, even though ten of the twelve men in the group had been referred for treatment by court order after having been found guilty of wife assault, and all of them had experienced problems with anger and violence, Robert made them nervous.

"What are you feeling right now?" I asked him.

He shrugged and said, "I don't know, not really anything . . . nothing, I guess."

I invited the other men in the group to describe how they experienced him. They told him he looked scared, depressed, and upset, and that he made them edgy and uptight. He was surprised to hear this.

It took about three weeks before Robert would talk about the violence that had led to his being in the group. The trouble started at his wife's office party. About thirty people were drinking and chatting when, according to Robert, Carol "disappeared"—he could not find her in the large, unfamiliar house where the party was being held. When he finally did locate her after ten to fifteen minutes, he insisted that they leave the party.

I asked him what he had been feeling at this point.

After a pause he said, "Nothing."

They drove home, she went to bed, and he began to watch television.

His next memory was of her lying in a pool of blood on the floor of their bedroom. He called her relatives and the police. Their report said that when asked what happened, he replied, "I must have hit her." He pleaded guilty in court, saying only, "I must have done it." When I inquired about the time period between watching television and seeing Carol covered in blood, he drew a blank. He said, "I believe I must have hit her but I can't remember doing it."

At that time, I surmised that shame had clouded Robert's memory. Now I know that something else was going on—a type of dissociative rage state that accompanies the enormous physical arousal inherent in a violent episode. Back in his "normal" state, Robert really couldn't remember what had happened; he never stored the memory of the incident.

Carol remembered, though. "I was asleep when he grabbed me," she revealed in a private interview. "He pulled off the covers and then yanked me out of bed by my hair. The light was on in the bedroom and I could see his face. . . . It was terrifying. His expression was distorted, contorted really. His mouth was frozen down at both corners like a fish mouth, his teeth were clenched, his jaw protruding, his nostrils flaring, and his eyes, well they were sort of bugged out and blank. He started to punch me with his fist, first on my stomach and side, then in my face. And he was yelling, 'You bitch, you cunt, you slut, you fucking whore!' That's all I remember."

It was at this point that Carol had lost consciousness.

As a result of the beating, Carol sustained a broken nose, a broken jaw, two chipped teeth, and bruised ribs. She was out of work for two months. Carol's mother told her office she had been in a car accident. Only her parents, sister, and two female friends knew what had really happened. Robert didn't want to tell anybody.

In treatment, Robert eventually disclosed that he believed his wife was having an affair and that when she "disappeared" at the party she was engaged in sex with a male coworker. In reality, however, she was talking to two female associates on an outside balcony. When we asked him where he imagined this intercourse was taking place in a crowded party, he said, "I don't know, in a car or something."

Then Robert explained that he would have what he called "red outs" when he got angry and couldn't remember what happened after that. "It was," he said, "like drowning in a red tide."

■ My Introduction into the Universe of Wife Abuse

How is it that someone can develop a need of this magnitude for another person, a need so great that it obliterates the ability to see the other as a human being, with her own wants and her own life? How is it that rage can overtake one so?

I grew up in a world where men like Ike Turner and O. J. Simpson and Robert didn't exist, or so I thought—a world that now seems a distant memory. I never witnessed anyone being beaten, not even slapped, at least not in my family or among my casual friends. My father was a gentle man who rarely raised his voice to his family, and never his hand.

It wasn't until many years after I left home that I discovered his own father had been abusive. My dad never talked about it when I was growing up, nor, for that matter, did he ever really talk about my grandfather at all. All I knew was that something was wrong between them. My dad had had to drop out of school to help support the family when he was sixteen; his father had a "drinking problem" and had abandoned him and his mother. I did ask a few questions, but they were met with terse answers and averted eyes. I quickly learned not to ask.

I didn't know about abuse in families or question why some kids left home early. Everybody said they were probably just "wild." Years later, when I was a young Ph.D. teaching academic social psychology on aggression, I faithfully lectured my students about the textbook studies on aggression toward enemies or strangers, but never questioned why there were no reports of aggression toward intimates. In those days, family violence was a well-kept secret. It happened, but no one talked about it—apparently not even research psychologists.

My introduction to wife abuse came in a strange and roundabout way. In 1974, I took a leave of absence from my job as a professor of forensic psychology at the University of British Columbia to work on a project modernizing police training. For two years I spent every Friday night riding on patrol with the local police department. I saw violence and death, and I learned that one of the duties police officers dread most was intervening in what they called "domestic disputes."

The first night I went out on patrol, Ron and Jim, the officers I accompanied, kept apologizing because things were slow. It was a Friday, however, the traditional night for domestic assault. Sure enough, around 10:00 P.M., the radio started to buzz. One call was from a nearby household. We took it.

We played it by the book, approaching cautiously, standing to either side of the door so no shotgun blast could hit us, and knocking loudly. A man answered the door. He was plainly drunk, slurring his words and lurching about. The cops told him they had a call about a family argument that had gotten out of hand.

"Is there anyone else in the house?" Ron wanted to know.

"Yes," the man replied.

"Can we come in?" The man hesitated. "Look," Ron continued, "we have to come in on a possible family trouble call. If there's no problem we'll be on our way."

The man relented. Ron started to ask him what was going on, focusing the man's attention on himself while Jim went to look for the woman who had called. I scuttled in behind the cops and tried to look inconspicuous. The house was trashed: tables overturned, clothing strewn on the living room floor, a bottle smashed in the kitchen. The man started to mumble about "having a little argument. My woman won't keep the house clean and is spending all my money. Work is hard, the hours too long."

Jim emerged from the back of the house with the woman who had called. When she saw her husband, she lunged at him, yelling, "You son of a bitch—"

The man yelled back, "Don't you—"

Jim escorted the woman into another room and asked her to sit down. She said, "Ralph beat me up and smashed up the place. He's my husband, he's done this before, and I'm afraid of him."

Back in the living room, Ralph overheard his wife's story. "What are you saying?" he yelled through the walls. "Why are you lying like this?"

Procedure in those days called for sitting both parties down, calming them, and trying to find out what had happened. Ralph was directed to an easy chair in the living room. Ron and Jim stationed themselves on the chair and sofa arms, ready to spring to their feet if hostilities resumed. The wife returned to the living room. She was not intimidated at all. In fact, she decided to let Ralph have it, describing drinking-abuse binges and how he had slapped her around, sworn at her, and called her a lazy whore. The cops were taking her statement.

Suddenly Ralph reached down under the easy chair cushion and pulled out a long knife. He was only six inches out of the chair when both cops hit him full force, grabbing the knife hand and twisting. They handcuffed him instantly and called the patrol wagon. Ralph was charged with common assault and assault with a deadly weapon. It was still only 10:45.

I remember another violent incident—actually its aftermath— some weeks later: a woman lying in the rain, dead, stabbed by her husband. I will never forget the look of shock and surprise on her face, the blood trickling down a slow incline, mixing with the rain, and running to a sewer grate twelve feet away; the red lights of the police cars rotating through the fog; the cops telling morbid jokes.

I wouldn't let myself feel anything for a month after that. Gradually, I learned why cops used humor that way.

The policemen I worked with were unhappy with the prospect of having to learn how to separate warring spouses, talk an angry man down, allow a distraught woman to weep, or comfort frightened kids. This was social work, they said. Their job was to be on patrol, in the streets getting ready for a bust. We pointed out that a lot of serious violence occurs indoors, in families. Wasn't that why they had joined the force, to reduce violence?

Still, our program enjoyed some success. Our goal was to help the police control the volatility and rage that could flare up unexpectedly. In following up on the policemen we had trained to handle "domestics," we learned that they felt more in control in those difficult family situations when compared to policemen who had not received the training.[3]

Arrest rates in cases of wife abuse, however, did not rise even with this extra training. I believed that they were far too low. Indeed, researchers at Indiana University had documented wife assaults that were occurring even while the police were present, but still the perpetrators were not arrested.[4]

In those days, that was due in part to a catch-22. Even if arrests occurred, judges rarely sent these men to prison, so why bother arresting them? reasoned the police. The judges felt little good would come of throwing domestic violence cases in with hardened criminals. Besides, they assumed imprisoning the offending husband would add enormous financial stress to the family and could exacerbate retaliatory violence after release. They just didn't know how to deal with wife abusers, so they did nothing.

However, one innovative judge in Vancouver was willing to experiment with new programs. Rather than imprisoning these men for months on end, he sentenced them to weekends in jail. After all, weekends were when they were most likely to reoffend, and this form of punishment didn't interfere with the men's ability to earn a living.

My colleague, therapist Dale Trimble, and I thought it might be useful to help these men learn to deal constructively with their anger. In 1978, sensing the criminal justice system had no effective means of rehabilitating men convicted of wife assault, we established a group therapy treatment program for these individuals. We were the first in Canada to do so, following closely on the pioneering work of Anne Ganley, whose methods we studied at American Lake V.A. Hospital in Tacoma, Washington.

■ A Glimpse into the World of the Batterer

The men who were referred to our treatment groups usually had never been in psychotherapy before and had thought it was for "sissies." Sent by the courts, they would rage and cry in their opening-night anxiety, some storming out, others attacking the justice system or their wives' actions that had "caused" their violence. Others broke into tears of self-recrimination and remorse.

These men seemed so normal. It wasn't until we interviewed their wives and heard about the insults, the gushing torrents of invective, and the beatings that we realized the horror of their home lives.

I was confused. While these certainly weren't "madmen," I also knew that most men were not abusive the way these batterers had been. What made them different? What special blend of social and psychological experiences brewed in their chemistry to produce violence toward their wives?

That was sixteen years and eleven hundred cases of wife assault ago. Since then, I have provided therapy for more than six hundred men. I have stepped inside their homes, their lives, their misery. I have conducted research with seven hundred abusers (both in and out of the therapy groups).

My search for answers took me through and beyond theories of violence in psychology and psychiatry. I undertook numerous scientific investigations of the personality profiles of abusive men; I used videotapes of couples arguing to elicit the abusers' reactions and conducted detailed examinations of their emotional reactions. I documented their wives' reports of their words and actions. And I spent innumerable hours in group therapy with them.

I have interviewed countless others, both perpetrators and victims, in private therapy and as clients in court cases for everything from child custody to murder. I have worked for the prosecution in some cases and the defense in others, and throughout, I have systematically made notes, collected data, formed and revised theories, and pondered and written numerous research papers for academic journals, as well as a book for academic use.

As the men gave up their secrets, I began to learn that intimate abuse was not just about hits and punches. It was about psychologically and physically trying to control their victims' use of time and space in order to isolate them from all social connection, both past and present. It was an all-out attempt to annihilate their wives' self-esteem, to enslave them psychologically. And it was performed repeatedly in order to maintain and inflate the damaged self-identity of the abuser. "The passion to have absolute and unrestricted control over a living being," as Eric Fromm put it so succinctly, "is the transformation of impotence into omnipotence."[5]

I have served as a group therapist long enough to have seen it all, or most of it, anyway. I've seen wives, wearing heavy makeup and dark glasses to hide the bruises, burst into tears during our private meetings. I've treated men who deny committing any violence but whose wives are hospitalized with broken arms and ribs "from an accident," and women who want to give their husbands "one more chance" after thirty previous assaults. I've seen a woman who got out of her hospital bed to marry the guy who put her there, and a police officer who would only take group treatment if we didn't reveal his line of work to the other men in the group. I've seen doctors, roofers, gardeners, hair stylists, loggers, bus drivers, men from every walk of life and ethnicity, all with one thing in common: They abused and hit the women they said they loved.

I've seen men stop their violence, men whom I never would have believed could do it, and I've seen others slip back to their old ways. I've written this book to explain my understanding of the answers to the many questions I've had to grapple with in the course of my experience with wife batterers.

■ Provocative Patterns

The more I studied and counseled these men, the more certain behavior patterns began to emerge, and the more I needed to understand the profile of a batterer. Indeed, as I became engrossed in this work, it triggered a flood of questions in me—questions that could only be answered through scientific research, further study, and interactions with the abusers themselves. And each answer gave rise to new questions.

Early on, it became clear that delusions of impending abandonment were a precursor to battering behavior. As in Robert's case, these seemed to be an immediate cause or "trigger" of intimate rage.

In her book, *Nicole Brown Simpson: The Private Diary of a Life Interrupted*, Faye Resnick, a personal friend of the murder victim, describes her experience of O. J. Simpson's jealous rages. Resnick reports that once, when the couple attempted a reconciliation, Simpson forced Nicole to confess who her lovers were during their separation. When one of these men entered a restaurant, Resnick reported, "Sweat poured down his face. The veins in his neck bulged. His cheekbones bunched up, twitching beneath his skin." And further, "O. J. treated her like his prize possession. He would fly into jealous rages if he even thought another man was looking at her."[6]

I wondered how the reaction that Resnick described, which psychiatrists call *conjugal paranoia* or *morbid jealousy*, originally developed and how the anxiety that fed them was converted into rage. What is this terror of being abandoned? How does it originate?

Escalating their abuse when they sensed an imagined abandonment, many abusive men I studied would drive their women away. Often this "sense" was based on a fiction, a misreading of signals. They created, in effect, the self-fulfilling prophecy of their worst nightmare. Others, having already been left by their wives, put them under surveillance, instigating a nightwatch on their residence or the transition house where they sought temporary shelter. Such men become a type of "stalker" and are potentially dangerous. One study found that 45 percent of *femicides* (murders of women) were generated by the man's "rage over the actual or impending estrangement from his partner."[7] It seemed to me that abandonment (whether real or imagined) had to be incorporated into any explanation of intimate male violence.

I wondered too about the strong sexual themes in these abandonment fantasies and whether they came from cultural messages or some deeper equation relating sex to attachment and loss. The men never framed the abandonment in terms of needing the woman and depending on her and her emotional support. Instead, they always reduced the scenario to a sexual triad: She was seeing someone else. Although the women were only rarely unfaithful, their husbands collected bits of "evidence": She dressed up that morning for work. She looked too good. What about the fifteen minutes she couldn't account for?

One man checked his wife's underwear in the laundry hamper, looking for "signs." When she disclosed this to me in therapy, he claimed she was having an affair with me and wrote to my psychological association. His "evidence" was that a bedroom was adjacent to the therapy room.

Another man flew into such rages whenever his girlfriend received a phone call from a man that she became traumatized by the phone. When it rang while I was interviewing her, she flinched. She described how, in her lover's mind, she had become a slut, a whore. The waves of woman-hatred poured off him. He broke into a sweat, the veins in his neck bulged. "He looked," she said, "like a wild man." She became terrified. With good reason.

Even men who were otherwise fairly "liberated" or egalitarian in their gender attitudes suddenly turned into obtuse male chauvinists when sexual suspicion was the theme. Where did this come from?

There's much to be learned from the language of cursing. When we're enraged and swearing at someone, the unguarded content reveals how we construe that person's worst side (and our own worst fears). Abused women inevitably say that men use the same four words when swearing at them: *bitch, cunt, whore, slut.* All are sexual, and all are related to her imagined lasciviousness. Why do virtually all abusive men use these expressions to degrade their partners? Why do most only repeat them in private? Is a societal double standard at work, or is this something deeper? How do men learn to swear at women, and how do they learn to humiliate?

The assault of wives typically occurs under specific circumstances (at home, in private) and times (upon someone's return home or late at night). Why is that so? The research data on wife assault suggest this is not at all a random act. Something more is going on that guides the direction or the focus of rage, something learned about male-female relationships.

Why does one man become jealous over events that are meaningless to another? When Robert perceived that his wife was "missing" at the office party, he assumed she was having sex somewhere. Would most men make that assumption? I don't think so. How do these individual differences originate? Even if two men become equally jealous, they don't necessarily become angry. Some get depressed as well as jealous. Why the emotional variation? In fact, if we examine men closely we will see that they vary greatly in terms of their arousability, jealousy when aroused, and anger when jealous.[8]

Even if they are angry, how they express the anger varies. Some men simply stifle it, others direct it toward themselves, others toward a third party, still others toward their female partner.

With all the talk about abusive relationships these days, it's easy to lose sight of the fact that most men[9] remain nonviolent toward intimate female partners over the course of their lifetime. Why do some men become violent and some not? Were they not all raised under the same socializing influences in the same society?

While it's relatively simple to learn how to make a fist and strike a blow, the intricacies of emotional abusiveness seem much more complex. At whose knee did abusive men learn how to find their partner's weak point, when this varies from one person to the next? How do they know what her vulnerabilities are? Did their fathers exploit their mothers the same way?

Is it a calm and deliberate monitoring of the self that determines the private quality of abusiveness? Or do two separate personalities develop, one for public and one for intimate relationships? Are some people basically the same in public and in private while others have a split so that two different sides of their personalities are manifested? Why do phases of violence exist and why do they occur so dramatically only in intimate relationships?

I wanted to explain these behaviors in men: men with whom I would work as a therapist for the next fifteen years. Men whose friends and neighbors thought they were "a nice guy—a little edgy sometimes—but basically a good fella." Men whose violence and rage were directed solely toward their wives. Men who, despite what might be taught in undergraduate psychology, had more than one personality—a Dr. Jekyll sweet, apparently caring side, intermittently supplanted by the dark Mr. Hyde.

■ Why Study the Psychology of Batterers?

I was driven to this study because I understand that wife abuse takes a terrible toll on all of society, not just on the women and men and children who are immediately gripped by its drama. The costs of policing and prosecuting, of medical care and missed workdays run into the hundreds of millions of dollars and are shared by all.

A study in Boston, for example, found that a substantial number of all women admitted to urban emergency rooms are victims of domestic violence.[10] Other researchers estimate that domestic homicide costs $1.7 billion a year. Because assaults are underreported, their true costs are harder to estimate.[11] Of course, these dollars and cents figures do not factor in the emotional and physical suffering.

And the problem is widespread. In 1975, Murray Straus, a family sociologist at the University of New Hampshire, and his colleagues Richard Gelles and Suzanne Steinmetz implemented the first national survey of family violence. As the powerful and revealing opening paragraph of their book, *Behind Closed Doors*, put it, "Drive down any street in America. More than one household in six has been the scene of a spouse striking his or her partner last year. . . . Every American neighborhood has violent families."[12]

Until the mid-1970s, these figures were hardly known. With a national sample of 2,143 respondents from intact families, the authors showed that family violence was not specific to any one race, social class, or neighborhood—it was ubiquitous. In about 24 percent of families, one spouse had pushed, grabbed, or shoved the other at some point in the marriage, 10 percent had kicked, bitten, or punched their spouses, and 6 percent had beaten up their spouses. Furthermore, 1.7 million Americans had at some time faced a husband or wife wielding a knife or gun.[13]

And the problem has not disappeared. In 1993, for example, there were 42,958 domestic violence calls in Los Angeles alone. About 2.5 million cases of battering occur each year, but, as I'll explain in Chapter 2, not all of those qualify as serious. On the other hand, some do. About two thousand incidents of wife abuse a year become murder cases.

During the pretrial hearings of the O. J. Simpson case, I was asked about the link between wife abuse and murder. I believe that these acts coexist on a continuum of domestic violence. In six different retrospective studies, jealousy, estrangement, and/or a history of physical abuse were the main precipitating factors to wives being murdered.[14] I cited studies in which investigators, beginning with a coroner's report, traced the path of abuse back through police records, friends, and family members to discover as much as they could about relationships that ended in murder.

In a Canadian investigation, half of the murdered women were killed by men who knew them intimately; one-quarter were killed during a period of estrangement from those men. The police had received prior calls for intervention in 65 percent of these femicides.[15] When researchers in Detroit and Kansas City tracked intimate homicides by address on a computer, they found previous police intervention had occurred in 90 percent of the cases.[16]

Is there some way to detect and intervene with these men before their violence becomes so extreme? From my experience, with appropriate therapy that addresses the perpetrator's real needs and underlying issues, it is possible for most wife abusers to change their ways and cease their violence. The prevention of further abuse and continued mental and physical anguish in themselves renders the study of these men more than worthwhile.

■ Perpetrator or Victim?

It's easy, given the atrocities against battered wives, simply to dismiss abusers as less than human or to see all men as inherently violent, as suffering from, as some call it, "testosterone poisoning." But if we do that, we draw a firm battle line between male and female, viewing all females as the victims of intimate abuse and all males as the perpetrators. And drawing those lines limits our ability to understand.

To perceive the male as both a victim and perpetrator confuses this compartmentalized view, and yet I believe that this more complex perspective reflects the reality of abusiveness. There is evidence that the abusive men whom you will meet in this book were once victims, too. Perhaps not solely victims of physical or sexual abuse, although that happens all too frequently, but of more subtle emotional droughts and demands that create a personality whose tendencies toward violence are exacerbated by social conditioning. Their victimization does not excuse their behavior, but it does explain it.

Only by fully understanding the origins of abuse will we have a chance to reduce it. It's a powerful experience for abusive men to come into a treatment group that holds them fully accountable for their actions; that does not, as the court may, diminish their responsibility because they were drinking that night; that demands they stop their destructiveness; that resists judging their actions but allows their inner self-condemnation to surface.

All the case histories in this book have been drawn from my treatment groups. It was in these groups that I heard how powerless these men felt in their lives, especially in their intimate relationships. Most don't know how to even describe a feeling to themselves, let alone assert it to an intimate other. Some men, it seems, could listen to the blues every day for a decade before they could verbalize their own grief. They could brag of sexual conquest before they could talk of deep loneliness or their addiction to "hits" of intimacy through physical contact with a woman. It is in recognizing this emotional self-alienation that we can understand the darkest side of the male sex role.

In the chapters to come, I will explore these facets of abusiveness. I will examine the various types of abusers and elucidate the predictable pattern of behavior known as the cycle of abuse. I will retrace the creation of the abuser's personality, surveying his father's and mother's contributions. I will explain the role of violence in the home of origin and demonstrate how a nascent batterer becomes a full-fledged perpetrator during adolescence. These early traumas contribute to the violence-prone borderline personality, a personality that learns to use violence to keep itself intact. Finally, I will conclude by describing the treatment of abusiveness. As a "fly on the wall" at a group, you will see how treatment succeeds and for whom it fails.

And in the end, you will understand how Robert could be swept away into the oblivion of a red tide of rage and how O. J. Simpson, the beloved idol of millions, could have beaten and degraded his comely ex-wife. These events are not mysteries. They have a source. And I will show it to you.

2 Are All Batterers Alike?

No, all batterers are not alike.

Sometimes it's a question of degree. Although surveys have shown that there are 2.5 million wife assaults in the United States each year,[1] not all of these are of the same gravity. The scale used to measure these events, the Conflicts Tactics Scale, developed by Murray Straus at the University of New Hampshire, includes a question such as: *Have you ever pushed, grabbed or shoved; slapped, kicked, bit, hit with a fist or an object; beat up; threatened with a knife or gun; or used a knife or gun against your partner?* There is a progression of violence here, but an answer of "yes" to any of these stages would, according to this scale, constitute assaultive behavior.

This is somewhat misleading. For example, if *once* in his marriage a man happens to push his wife in reaction to situational stresses, he would still be considered abusive according to the Conflicts Tactics Scale. But, psychologically, that is a very different type of individual than one who repeatedly abuses or beats up his wife or engages in more serious assaults. To me, it's like the distinction between a single fender bender and continual head-on collisions. About 2 percent of the population would qualify as habitual batterers.

But we can't limit our definition to purely physical acts. Some men assault their wives emotionally by dominating or isolating them, controlling their use of time and space, and monitoring their expenditures.

In her book, Faye Resnick describes the control techniques that O. J. Simpson used:

> First, he told Nicole not to see guys or have them in the house, even if they were just friends; second, he made her sneak cigarettes, making her feel bad about herself . . . ; third, he told her she couldn't go out dancing with her girlfriends unless he was out of town, or spend too much time with them; fourth, he convinced our men to control their women and keep them at home more, thereby effectively isolating Nicole; and fifth, he started trying to control Nicole's family again by throwing them financial rewards.[2]

O. J.'s "molding" of Nicole began when she was seventeen. He was obsessed with her body image, abusing her verbally for being too fat when she became pregnant and insisting that she have her breasts cosmetically enlarged.

Habitual batterers may verbally abuse their wives, humiliating, shaming, and cursing them. The latter are attempts at undermining the woman's self-esteem and make her more "manageable."

Emotional and physical abuse are significantly related to one another. Both are based on a need for control and domination. Incidents of physical violence may be widely spaced, while other forms of emotional abuse are occurring in the interim.

When one of my clients, Jon, beat his wife in 1985, he had warned her, "Next time, it's going to be worse." Marge reported that Jon's face contorted into a mask of rage during the assault. Consequently, whenever she recognized that expression, she immediately toed the line. Jon continued to control and abuse

Marge emotionally, even though the next incident of physical battering occurred six years later.

Although I cannot say that there is a progression from emotional assault to physical assault—the first doesn't necessarily lead to the other—it is true that a physical assault can also be considered an emotional assault. We all react with shame and outrage at being hit.

About 30 percent of all habitually assaultive men behave in the way that my client Robert does.[3] I call these individuals cyclical/emotionally volatile abusers.

These men are not constantly violent, but periodically so. Many of their partners describe their recurring metamorphosis: they transform from a kindly Dr. Jekyll personality to a terrifying Mr. Hyde. Although they are frequently buddies with men and unlikely to display any anger with them, their predominant rage is with the woman to whom they're emotionally connected. Indeed, this woman becomes a lightning rod for all the emotional storms in their lives.

Others describe a specific triggering event that brings on the beating—a real or imagined move toward leaving the relationship, even a pregnancy. The imagined "abandonments" are more frequent, much like Carol and Robert's experience the night of the office party.

Furthermore, these men are abusive only within the confines of the relationship and the abuse occurs repeatedly in spite of what the women may do: pleading, cajoling, reasoning, fighting back make little difference. Nevertheless, according to Murray Straus's surveys, about one-third of the men who assault their wives stop spontaneously, without police involvement.[4] Why this happens is unknown. Perhaps some women convince their husbands that they will leave, or perhaps the men have become too upset about their actions.

Most of my research has been with the cyclical abuser, and the remainder of this book is devoted to them. But not all men who assault their wives have a cyclical personality. Let's look briefly at the other kinds of abusive men, since the cyclical batterer is but one of three general types.

■ Psychopathic Wife Assaulters

Lenny was a psychopath—not that you'd know it right off. He seemed somewhat perturbed that he was late to his initial interview. "The bus broke down," he explained breathlessly as he settled into his chair. "I'm glad to finally get this treatment started. I'd wanted to do it for years. Maybe if I'd had it years ago, things might have been different," he said with a smile. Lenny was charming and ingratiating, boyish and attractive. I wanted to like him; he saw to that.

Nevertheless, there was something indefinably cold about him. I couldn't quite put my finger on it. Lenny had grown up in the suburbs and had run with a gang. As a juvenile, he had gotten into trouble for setting fires, stealing autos, selling drugs, and fighting in school. He asked me if he'd seen me on television—I had appeared on a daily national show for three years—and then, illogically, told me how much he liked the show. "I'm really interested in psychological issues," he said. "I'm going back to school to get a psychology degree." He had dropped out of high school after the tenth grade.

Lenny had a long rap sheet: breaking and entering, petty theft, burglary, and armed robbery. "I'm going to put all that behind me," he said. "I want to make a brand new start, to, you know, 'give back' to the world. I'm sick of the fixation society has with cheap thrills, with surface glitter. I want a relationship with substance, maybe with a woman and kids."

Lenny had had nine relationships with women in the previous three years. He'd been violent in at least three relationships that I knew of. His criminal career started with stealing his mother's jewelry. He said he had never really known her. He left home at fifteen. "The people I stole from were insured anyway," he explained. "They never suffered. The only one who suffered was me. The woman I hit had it coming. She had a bad drug habit and was sleeping around. I warned her to quit the drugs. I was trying to go straight, and she was stopping me. Now she's not around to get in my way. . . ."

And on and on it went. No remorse. No looking back. Only a relentlessly unrealistic view of the future.

About 40 percent of the men who come to our treatment groups meet the diagnostic criteria for antisocial behavior[5]—that is, they have a history of criminal activities. Antisocial behavior was once thought to be indicative of psychopathy, but in his book *Without Conscience: The Disturbing World of the Psychopaths Among Us*, my colleague Robert Hare, who has studied psychopaths for more than twenty years, has noted that while they do typically engage in criminal activities, they also have a more central and psychological defining feature: a lack of emotional responsiveness that sets them apart from other criminals.[6]

Hare describes this as missing conscience. Conscience is the ability to punish the self for violating one's own standards of conduct. Most normally socialized men who are not psychopathic do go through some remorse for hurting their wives. The pangs of guilt are painful, so they find ways to neutralize the self-punishment by mentally reconstructing the reprehensible action—often by blaming the victim for having provoked it ("I told her not to make me angry. If she hadn't nagged me . . . ") or an outside factor such as alcohol. Sometimes they will minimize the act through the language they employ to describe it ("the night we had our little incident") or they'll make comparisons to others ("Most men are as violent as I am").

But psychopaths have no such pangs. In fact, Hare has found that their brains do not function like those of normal people when they are observing emotionally provocative events. MRI (magnetic resonance imaging) brain scans performed on psychopaths and normal men show dramatically different processing. The MRI for psychopaths look as though nothing is happening—just a bit of bright color in the brain stem area toward the back of the brain, indicating glucose metabolism and brain activity.

"I showed these slides to a group of doctors," Hare told me in his lab, "and they laughed. They said the patient must be nearly dead."

By contrast, the scans of the normal men revealed huge color patterns radiating from the brain stem forward to the temporal lobes—an indication of extensive brain activity.

The psychological syndrome of psychopathy includes the loss of the ability to imagine another person's fear or pain or the dreadful consequences that might follow abuse. Other key signs of psychopathy include shallow emotional responses and an unrealistic future scenario (such as Lenny's plan to study psychology) accompanied by an unwillingness to examine past problems.

How are psychopaths created? That's unclear. Hare claims that he can find no "convincing evidence that psychopathy is the direct result of social or environmental factors."[7] He theorizes that it's a genetic condition. Others believe, however, that it has a psychological basis. Psychiatrist John Bowlby, for example, thought of psychopathy as a form of extreme "detachment" resulting from an infant having its early needs for intimacy and closeness chronically frustrated.[8] And psychologist Dan Saunders of the University of Michigan has found that generally violent men who have been the most severely abused when growing up are the most extremely abusive toward their wives.[9]

Unlike cyclical abusers, however, psychopathic batterers such as Lenny are often violent with others as well as their partners. Moreover, they are frequently arrested for nonviolent crimes such as forgery, passing bad checks, or confidence rackets. These actions are hallmarks of a so-called antisocial lifestyle.

When psychopaths are referred to treatment groups for wife assault, they are considered a poor bet for improvement. Psychopaths don't look back. As a result, they never learn from past mistakes.

Psychologist Neil S. Jacobson has identified a subgroup of psychopathic men whom he calls "vagal reactors." (*Vagal* refers to the vagus nerve, which conducts impulses between the brain and the muscles of the throat, heart, and abdomen.) Usually when we're upset, we experience an autonomic response: our hearts race, our palms become sweaty, our breathing turns quick and shallow, our stomachs churn. Vagal reactors don't respond in this way. In fact, their internal reactions become cool and controlled when they are engaged in heated arguments with their wives.

As Jacobson put it in his 1993 keynote address to the American Association of Marriage and Family Therapy,

> We were astonished to find that about 20 percent of our batterers actually showed a decline in heart rate during the course of the nonviolent argument. In other words, some of these batterers became calm internally despite their emotionally aggressive behavior. This disconnection between physiology and behavior was something none of us had ever observed, and it makes no intuitive sense. They look aroused, they act aroused, but on the inside they are getting calmer and calmer.
>
> Furthermore, the batterers who showed this heart rate decrease were the most belligerent and contemptuous toward their wives. . . . The "disconnected" group showed the highest rates of violence outside the marriage, and were the most likely to have reported violence in their family of origin.[10]

According to Jacobson, about 20 percent of all batterers and half of all antisocial personalities are vagal reactors.[11]

Vagal reactors might be the velociraptors of intimate violence. They function like trained martial artists, cool and composed, with a suppressed autonomic reaction while highly alert and tuned to the environment. As Jacobson explained, "instead of being out of control, our most severe subgroup of batterers were like 'autonomic athletes,' actively controlling their level of arousal so that they can focus their attention on their wives, presumably so that aggression can have the maximal effect."[12] Their violence is instrumental and controlled. It has the purpose of controlling and dominating the other person, and it is cunningly expressed to achieve this end.

■ Overcontrolled Wife Assaulters

About 30 percent of assaultive males are designated *overcontrolled*.[13] These men appear to be somewhat distanced from their feelings and on psychological tests show a strong profile of avoidance and passive-aggression. These are the guys who say they just want to be working on their cars; they can't understand what the fuss is all about. Their anger—usually a buildup of frustration to external events—can suddenly erupt in violence after long periods of seething but unexpressed rage.

For these reasons, overcontrolled wife assaulters have the lowest profile; they simply lack the flamboyant characteristics that attract media reports of violence. They are, in many ways, the mirror opposite of the stereotypical wife beater.

Two kinds of overcontrolled men exist. The *active type* is sometimes characterized as a "control freak" who extends his need for extreme domination to others. Wives of these men describe them as being meticulous, perfectionistic, and domineering. The *passive type* simply distance themselves from their wives, and the couples usually argue over the attainment of some emotional contact. Both types show up for treatment as apparently "good clients"—they are compliant and try hard to please the therapist.

On psychological tests that measure the maltreatment of women, overcontrolled men generate extremely high scores on one factor of abusiveness called dominance/isolation and on a second scale used most often to measure emotional abusiveness.[14] Dominance/isolation includes behavior in which the husband requires rigid observance of sex roles ("He becomes upset if the household work is not done when he thinks it should be"), demands subservience ("He acts like I'm his personal servant"), and isolates his wife from resources ("He refuses to let me work outside the home," "He restricted my use of the telephone," "He was stingy giving me money").

The emotional abuse includes verbal attacks ("He insults or shames me in front of others"), and the denial of emotional resources ("He withholds affection from me"). All forms of emotional abuse are coercive techniques to generate submission.

Laura knew only too well about the themes of dominance/isolation and emotional abuse. She was sitting in my office, embroiled in a legal battle, seeking my advice. I could see that she had been attractive before the years of brainwashing had taken their toll. She looked a little wizened now, as if some vital energy had been sucked from her. Laura had met Colin in 1976 and, according to her recollection, it was an odd pairing; she was a leftover "flower child" from the 1960s, working as a flight attendant, and he was a conservative airline pilot.

In some strange way, Colin reminded Laura of her father. She had grown up in a home that was paternalistic and traditional. Her mother obeyed her father. She found Colin's cool, calm manner appealing. He seemed always to be in control. At some level, Laura felt he would take care of her. After all, every time she flew with him, she had put her life in his hands, and he had always come through.

Laura repeatedly twisted a piece of paper as she recounted this to me. It was a small thing, but it gave her something to do with her trembling hands, and at least she could feel some sense of control over it. Control had become a very scarce commodity in her life.

She remembered Colin being "ornery" at times before their marriage. Her father distrusted him, but that, she believed, was only natural. Occasionally Colin would become verbally abusive, sarcastically criticizing Laura for how long it took her to get ready, or her forgetfulness, or her past as a hippie. But he would always be extra nice after these outbursts. Laura remembered thinking that he had a personality problem but that "at least he doesn't beat me."

The strength of the attraction to Colin was enough to make Laura try to overlook the "personality problem," as she called it. He would get over it in time, she thought, "once he really loves and trusts me."

They dated for two years in Seattle, lived together for a year, and then married on Valentine's Day 1978. Colin refused to meet her family, invited no one to the wedding, and picked out their wedding outfits and rings. She asked him few questions at the time; he had made it clear that he didn't want to answer any. In retrospect, she thought that he probably married because it seemed the proper social step. None of his friends were single.

After several months of marriage, Colin responded with anger and frustration at Laura's announcement that she was pregnant. He focused on their having to leave the adults-only apartment building in which they were living. He decided to relocate to the small town where he had grown up in eastern Washington because it was cheaper to live there. Of course, this also meant that Laura would have to give up her job as a flight attendant.

Once they had moved and Laura gave birth to a daughter, Colin decided that he needed an apartment in Seattle; it was more convenient for his flying schedule. By this time Laura was pregnant again. Colin returned to Seattle, phoned her every few days, and gave her a small allowance to raise the family and pay for groceries. He controlled all other finances.

In 1984, Colin bought some land about twenty miles from town and built a log house. He moved Laura and the kids there, gave her a four-wheel drive to get to town, and visited irregu-larly—sometimes every few weeks, but at other times not for three or four months. It had been a step by step process, but now Laura was totally isolated, had all her spending monitored, was allowed one call each month to her parents in Michigan, and had no medical coverage.

She tried to join a tennis club in town, but Colin never welcomed anyone to their place and was, in fact, surly and unfriendly to anyone she met. At the same time, he established an all-male network and was one of the boys.

When Laura discovered a letter to him from his mistress in Minneapolis, her humiliation forced a confrontation. He laughed in her face and told her she was ugly and unappealing. At that point, they hadn't had sex in two years. Laura went to see a lawyer and asked for a divorce. Colin talked her into staying for the sake of the children. She relented, telling herself that at least he wasn't around a lot and wasn't physically abusive. But that would soon change.

After a brief period of wooing her back, Colin's controlling behavior intensified. First he demanded that she bring itemized lists of household bills for his inspection. Then when Laura received a small inheritance, he convinced her to invest it in a company he was starting. Colin was uncomfortable with Laura having her own resources, accurately seeing it as a form of independence. She had no credit cards and had to ask him for money, accounting for every cent.

Colin's emotional abuse worsened, too. Whenever Laura tried to establish some independence by taking a course at school, he accused her of abandoning the kids and being selfish. He told her she was a dilettante who would never amount to anything in the real world. He began to obsess over the kids being superstar figure skaters. His preoccupation with control shifted toward them.

The year before, Colin had started to drink and now was spending more time in the house with Laura, although they had separate bedrooms. He would bait her sarcastically and turn the kids against her, depicting her to them as a hysterical flake. He criticized her appearance, her mothering, her housekeeping, her parents, and her hippie past, systematically attacking her very essence. Then Colin started breaking into Laura's room at night, haranguing her about how her attempts to get social support were abdications of her mothering role. Some days he wouldn't let her leave the house, physically restraining her, threatening her with violence.

This is often the strategy of emotional abuse: attack the current social support, the connection to the past identity, and finally the current identity. It is a brilliant execution of brainwashing techniques—identical to those used in the Inquisition and the Korean War.

Laura became desperate to escape the harassment. When she finally broke free, she signed, out of desperation, a separation agreement that gave her minimal child support and only $20,000 to live on. Then, during a meeting to work out details of the agreement, Colin, in his words, "lost his cool" and struck her. Laura called the police.

Laura looked up at me toward the end of our interview. "It's really hard," she said, "when you're the one they're supposed to love."

The overwhelming sadness of that statement stayed with me. Laura blamed herself for not "seeing it sooner," but the incremental nature of the control, like a slowly tightening noose, obscured its onset. Her own background with a controlling father had not only prepared her, it had drawn her to a repetition of a lifelong struggle with a controlling man.

■ Cyclical/Emotionally Volatile Wife Abusers

I once read in a magazine the following statement attributed to a male movie star: A man wants to keep a woman like a snake on a stick with a noose around its neck so that he could move her closer or further at will. The sense of danger from too much closeness or distance struck me. The phrase spoke to the fear that cyclical/emotionally volatile abusers experience around intimacy: they feel either abandonment or engulfment.

My earliest work with these men focused on their inability to describe their feelings and their extreme need to control intimacy. We all need power in our lives but we don't all generate it by dominating others. I wondered if an inner sense of powerlessness created this preoccupation with external power—with control of another whom the abuser simultaneously views as essential and abhorrent.

Along with my graduate student Jim Browning, I began to experiment with the power motives of violent men and with their reactions to videotaped scenarios of couples arguing. In some of the scenes, the woman would attempt to distance herself from the man, in others she was trying to get closer. Other conflicts involved more everyday issues such as where to spend summer vacation.

I used projective tests, measuring the men's responses to assess their power motivation. I found that violent men needed to have an impact on others, especially an intimate other. These men got angriest in response to videos in which the woman was in control and moving away emotionally. The group of violent men became the angriest compared to other nonviolent groups of men while watching this scene.[15] Indeed, the violent men perceived more abandonment in the scene and reacted with more fear and anger to what they thought they saw.

I started to think about emotional distance as the most crucial issue to intimately violent men. Why, I still didn't know. The actor's quote stayed with me, though; we try to control those things that scare us the most. But if these men were so afraid of intimacy, why were they in relationships at all? What kept drawing them back? I frequently asked them these questions but they would only shrug and say, "I don't know." When they did proffer an explanation, it was usually in terms of reliability and creature comforts.

Over the years, however, I discovered that the cyclical/emotionally volatile abusers experience a constellation of feelings involving rage and jealousy. They find ways of misinterpreting and blaming their partners, holding them responsible for their own feelings of despondency, making impossible demands on them, and punishing them for inevitably failing. These men are held in the grip of cyclical moods that ebb and flow with a fearful rhythm.

Perhaps that is why their wives describe them as having dual personalities. I don't remember how many times I heard it before it dawned on me. But as I look now at the interview notes I took from partners of my clients, the phrases jump off the pages: "He's like two people." "His friends never see the other side of him. They think he's just a nice guy, just one of the boys." "I never know which one is coming in the door at night." I have more than two hundred files with the same statements, all offered spontaneously to my request for a description.

It wasn't just those phrases, but the sameness in the depiction of the cyclical abusers that seemed significant: always moody, irritable, jealous, changeable. As one woman put it, "He's living on an emotional roller coaster."

What's more, these men are highly innovative in their verbal abusiveness, indicating a perverse imagination that does not just copy but embellishes a theme. One man, for example, heaped scorn on his wife's abilities as a mother. When she returned to school, however, his abuse refocused on her as a student. "You're stupid. You'll never get anywhere. It's all a pipe dream," he would say. These men have a need to shame and humiliate another human being, to finally obliterate their own shame and humiliation. (See Chapter 5.) They also know exactly how hard to hit in order to scare and intimidate their wives without leaving marks.

Meyer was just such a man. Carla, his wife of ten years, came into my office looking composed and professional. She was a classic California blonde, tanned and fit, with her hair tied tightly in a bun. She was a large-boned, athletic woman who some might describe as aloof and icy. If she'd told me she had just retired from the professional tennis tour or was marketing fitness videos, I wouldn't have been surprised. She sat across from me with her arms folded and her legs crossed. She looked as though she was trying to protect herself from some invisible attacker. As she started to talk about Meyer, though, her image and her hair began to unravel.

Meyer had a law degree but didn't practice. Instead, he made his money in real estate. He had grown up in New York City, where he had gone to college and law school before moving west. He was a "schemer" she said, caught up in the adrenalin rush of his business with a maze of interlocking deals made at high speed on his cell phone.

They had met through a mutual friend and had had a whirlwind romance, getting married after four months. Soon, the problems started. Meyer loved to argue but couldn't stand it when he didn't win, complete with a verbal concession. When Carla wouldn't concede a point one night, he started to shake, called her a bitch, and stormed off. He went to bed, then came down to the TV room where she was sitting, and started hitting and kicking her repeatedly. Then he put his hands around her throat and began to strangle her. She escaped to a neighbor's house but refused to call the police. She couldn't believe the violence had really occurred, and the unreality paralyzed her.

When Carla tentatively returned home, Meyer was in bed in a fetal position, sucking his thumb and staring blankly at the wall.

I asked Carla, "Did anything unusual precede Meyer's abuse?"

"He got a phone call from his mother," she replied. "Whenever he talks to her, he gets angry with me about virtually anything. He would just pick an issue."

After this incident, the abuse and violence worsened. Over the years, Carla began to detect what she described as a six-week cycle. At first Meyer was fine. Then he became withdrawn and more argumentative. He would obsess about money even though he had millions. Toward the end, he would become unbearable, like a summer heat wave. She would wait for the thunderstorm to relieve the heat.

As his tension mounted, he would escalate his complaints about her spending. He couldn't tolerate her having close friends, so he would begin to find fault with them. Then, he would focus on her, calling her a whore and a slut. As she put it, "He calls me a whore because he only wants someone to share his bed." He would yell at her to get out, and when she packed her bags, he would beg her to stay.

Once, they were driving to another town in his car. As usual, he was upset about money. An argument ensued. Meyer pulled over and started beating Carla. She ran out of the car into the woods beside the highway. He continued on, abandoning her. She stumbled into a trailer park, where she found someone to take her home. She was physically hurt for days; her shoulder and breast were black and blue.

At this point, it occurred to Carla that her husband could kill her. She returned to California for a while with their eight-year-old son and entered psychotherapy. Her main concern was why she couldn't leave Meyer. She felt guilt about her own dependence, made worse when their son, who was in therapy with her, asked, "Mom, why do you stay with daddy if he beats you?" and then suggested, "I would rather be alone with you than with someone who might kill us."

Both her therapist and her pastor pushed her to get tough and to set conditions for her return to Meyer. She decided on his agreeing to stay in therapy (at least twice a week) and to consult weekly with his clergyman. Meyer had previously quit therapy three times with female therapists who confronted him.

Meyer and Carla reunited just before his fortieth birthday. He awakened her the night of his birthday and started to stammer as he always did when he was anxious. He told her he was unhappy and wanted a divorce. Then, in a whirl of contradictions, he said he wanted to remarry right away and would never hit Carla again. He immediately began slapping her. Grabbing a portable phone, she locked herself in a closet and dialed 911.

When the police showed up, Carla was hysterical and Meyer appeared calm and collected. He told the cops that they had been having a marital squabble and that he was really embarrassed they were called. He said that Carla was emotionally volatile because she was approaching menopause.

The cops were suspicious, especially since she told them that she had been hit. They looked for bruises or scratches, but could find none. Meyer had not smacked her hard enough for welts to show. He was playing up to the police perfectly, respecting their authority, ostensibly cooperating, trying to "recruit" them by forming a male coalition where the common grievance was hysterical females.

"Does your wife ever get like this?" he asked disingenuously.

The cops finally decided that, in the absence of any visible injuries, they would not charge. They let Meyer off with a warning.

Toward the end of our interview, Carla, like so many other wives of cyclical/emotionally volatile abusers, looked up at me with tears in her eyes. "It's like Meyer is two people," she said. "One is very responsible to his family, the other could kill us."

Carla was now talking divorce, and the dollar signs began flying past Meyer's eyes. Perhaps to stall her, he referred himself to our treatment group. He seemed likable, articulate, cooperative, and self-aware.

But I wasn't fooled.

3 The Cycle of Violence and the Abusive Personality

EDDIE HAD BEEN IN A WORSENING MOOD FOR DAYS. He couldn't tell what started it, but it was probably something Cheryl had said. He was pissed at her. She was jerking him around. At first, it was just little thoughts racing across his mind. "She's a lousy housekeeper." "She drinks too much." "The sex is rotten." He felt himself distancing from her. When he looked at her, which was seldom these days, it seemed as if he were peering through the wrong end of a telescope. She was remote. He began to ignore her, disregarding her questions about everyday matters.

Then, although he hadn't noticed, the thoughts became more frequent and began to blot out his normal internal dialogue. Even when he was at work, he obsessed on what a bitch she was. They never made long-term plans anymore. That trip to Mexico they were going to take was off. When she had a long telephone conversation with her ex-husband, an image flashed across Eddie's mind so fast, he barely glimpsed it. In it, he was in high school and his mother was making fun of his weight. "You're so fat," she had said, "they'll give you a job in the circus. That's the only way you'll amount to anything." He was sensitive about his 300-pound bulk.

Eddie snidely remarked to Cheryl, "Maybe you should get back together with Jack, so you can talk all night."

"We're only trying to work out some arrangements about the kids," she replied.

The next day, he noticed her getting dressed up for work. Her outfit was too sexy. He knew she was seeing somebody.

Eddie worked as a cabbie, and that day he had no patience with drivers who cut him off. He got home before Cheryl and went through her underwear drawer, looking for evidence.

When he came to group that night, Eddie was clearly agitated. He started in on immigrant cab drivers, and how he had to live with them all day. "They can't drive worth shit," he griped. "They have their cousins pass the tests for them."

I pointed out to Eddie that he seemed to be wound pretty tight. I asked how things were going at home. He declared he was getting out of the relationship. "She's too fucked up. She can't get her act together. She's still using [heroin]. She'll never change. I feel like shit, and it's all because of her. I'm getting the hell out!"

Concerned by the warning signs, I called Cheryl the next day. "How has Eddie been?" I asked.

"Bad," she said. "He's getting into one of his moods. Withdrawn, negative, nothing is right. The other day he came home and complained that he didn't want to go out, that I was always pushing him to party. The plan for the evening had started with him; he wanted to see an old buddy! I know he's building for something, looking to pick a fight. You can feel the tension around here."

I reviewed with Cheryl her safety steps in case Eddie got worse: She was to ask him if he was upset, not take on his anger, and draw a clear line; she was to warn him if he threatened violence, lock herself into the bathroom (where she had installed a deadbolt on the inside), and call 911 from her cell phone if she was afraid he would blow.

Meanwhile, at work, Eddie was fantasizing about the company secretary. He could have her, if it weren't for Cheryl. Then he started to generalize: Not only did Cheryl cause his restricted lifestyle, but she was also the source of his misery, the reason for his deprived state. In reality, the secretary wasn't interested in Eddie, but even if she were, and they started a relationship, he would soon be blaming her for the same transgressions he now accused his wife of.

That night, after his shift, Eddie lit into Cheryl. "You look like shit lately, and the house is a mess. If I didn't take you in, you wouldn't have anyone." She tried staying calm, tried defusing him, to no avail. He was working himself up. He started yelling. "Why should I hustle all day to support a no-good whore like you?"

Cheryl could see the color in his face change to purple. He smashed his fist into the wall right beside her head. He lunged to grab her, but she twisted away. She ran into the bathroom and locked the door, but didn't call the police. He left.

When he came back several hours later, he was full of apologies. At group the following week, Eddie had nothing but high praise for his wife.

■ The Phases of Abuse

In 1979, psychologist Lenore Walker wrote *The Battered Woman*,[1] a classic text based on interviews with 120 abused women in Denver, Colorado. The book was the first of its kind, and became a seminal source for much of our current knowledge about this population. Indeed, the women's descriptions of the abuse experience later became the basis for Walker's developing the battered woman syndrome, and its subsequent use as a legal defense.

One aspect of the descriptions was of particularly great interest to me. The women described in detail a cyclical buildup of tension and abusive release that Walker referred to as the *battering cycle*. It consisted of three phases that could vary in timing and intensity for the same couple and from one couple to the next: tension-building, the explosion of acute battering, and loving contrition.

The wives of cyclical abusers whom I have seen in my practice corroborate this. They all complain that their husbands become irritable for no apparent reason. They go through building tension cycles that are unrelated to their surroundings. They react with escalating verbal and physical attacks. They are pathologically jealous, drawing ludicrous conclusions about nonexistent extramarital affairs. They don't merely react to events, but create a different view of the world in which emotional bumps become earthquakes. And then, suddenly, after the cataclysmic explosion, they are sweet and loving and gentle.

I have always been fascinated by these similarities among cyclical abusers' behavior patterns—even down to the words they use to humiliate their women. It's as though they all attended a regimented school and studied the same curriculum. Cyclical batterers are literally either at their wives' knees or at their throats.

THE PSYCHOLOGY OF THE TENSION-BUILDING PHASE

Usually, the tension buildup that leads the cyclical abuser into his Mr. Hyde personality is hidden from public view. His friends and coworkers rarely see the signs. If anything, they might notice that he's "a little moody" or "a bit tense." I call these subtle clues *leakage*.

Some leakage would occur in group sessions during Eddie's tension-building phase. He would seem, at first, more serious, preoccupied, edgy. He became distracted, as if he were somewhere else. He would complain more than usual about whatever ethnic group was on his emotional hit list for the week. Small issues assumed great importance, as if he were caught inside them and couldn't see their limits.

Most cyclical abusers experience a similar process whenever the darkness begins to overtake them. Profound fear and vulnerability are building behind the moodiness and preoccupation. As we will see in part 2, cyclical abusers have a fragile sense of self. Their anxiety about coming apart at the seams is accompanied by a heightening of uncomfortable feelings called *aversive arousal*. This is a state of irritating excitement: the individual is agitated, tense, frenzied; he can't sit still or relax and feels some inner force will overtake him. He would like to be rid of this condition at all costs, if only he could identify what *it* is.

Faye Resnick describes O. J.'s state of aversive arousal.[2] On one public occasion, when Resnick was present, Nicole mentioned the name of an ex-lover in casual conversation. Here is Resnick's description of what followed:

> O. J.'s charming face turned into a profile of rage. He turned to me and burst out, "What the fuck is she doing, Faye? Why does she have to go and ruin everything by saying that name? . . . " O. J.'s face twitched uncontrollably. His body language was extremely aggressive. Horrified, I watched as sweat poured down his face. The veins in his neck bulged. His cheekbones bunched up, twitching beneath his skin. He ground his teeth in rage and hissed at me, "Goddamned bitch! Why the fuck does she do this?"

It's one thing to read about aversive arousal and quite another to actually see it in the extreme. Resnick's description shows how strongly the mere mention of a potential rival can produce a severe reaction of jealous rage in an abusive man. According to Resnick, Simpson then followed her into the ladies' room, breaking the lock on the door, began urinating in her presence, and "cursing the mother of his children with a vengeance I'd never heard from anyone! I fled the room."[3]

Some abusive men experience these states in reaction to a "trigger." Others develop them internally without an external cause. Cyclical abusers operate in the latter way.

The cyclical abuser experiences the diffuse tension and vaguely senses that something is wrong, but can't find or never knew the words to name it. His emotional lexicon is too limited. When I started treating these men, I was struck by the repetitive aspect of their lives and relationships, the emotional poverty of their thought and speech, their flat affect, and noncommittal responses. The men described actions that people performed, but those rarely entered the inner emotional realm.

If I were to ask a cyclical abuser to describe his experience of aversive arousal, "bummed out" or "weird" might come to his mind. More likely, however, he'd draw a blank about himself. But his wife—she was another matter altogether.

Since males in our society are often conditioned to be sensitive to the external environment rather than to their emotions or interior states, they may simply pin the blame for their discomfort on someone else. If they were raised in a family that traditionally believes wives are responsible for their husbands' feelings, they may naturally and unselfconsciously blame their partners. This provides them an untroubling and socially sanctioned explanation for the apprehension. It also provides an excuse to get angry.

And so, over and over again in groups, rather than hearing, "I'm scared," "I feel like I'm falling apart," "I'm tense and anxious all over," I hear instead the externalization of blame for an inner state of unnamed anguish: "She doesn't dress the kids," "She doesn't keep the house clean," "She doesn't fix the meals." If she did, in the magical thinking of the abuser's mind, these strange bad feelings would disappear.

At this stage, cyclical abusers repeatedly play what we call in group "the bitch tape," a mental cassette stuck permanently on auto reverse. Side one has some version of: "I feel bad. It's her fault." Side two says: "She's a bitch. She's always putting me down."

Psychiatrists call the repetitive aspect of this self talk *rumination*. Cyclically abusive men obsess on this thought pattern of blame, bad feelings, and fantasized recrimination. Often these thoughts center on jealousy and sexual infidelity.

The cyclical abuser is terrified that his wife will abandon him. In my research with Jim Browning, in which we showed men videotapes of women arguing with their husbands for more independence, I found that abusive men are more sensitive to and perceive more abandonment than do nonabusive men. And, having done so, they react with elevated anger and anxiety to these scenes, especially if the women are winning the argument.[4]

Participants in my treatment groups are frequently irrationally jealous about their wives. Eddie's belief that his wife was having an affair is typical. These men monitor their wives' use of time and space, becoming suspicious of all contact with other men. They assume that all other men view their wives as desirable sexual objects.

Paradoxically, however, the men frequently talk about their abandonment fears while still trying to maintain a distanced, cool, or dismissing tone about their emotional dependence on their wives. In the beginning of treatment, they might complain about their wives' behavior, in part, as a way to deflect the focus from their own abusiveness. It's not unusual for a man who has been condemning his wife's worst habits to act surprised when asked, "So why do you stay with her, if she's so bad?" It's as if he has never considered that question. And his responses are typically flimsy and transparent.

What the cyclical abuser would never say is that he desperately needs his wife to define himself, finds himself irrevocably bound to her, and considers the prospect of being alone terrifying. This process is called *masked dependency*. The abuse keeps the woman in place while allowing the man to overlook his own hidden dependency needs and maintain his illusion of detachment.

Robert's experience was representative. The most innocuous events triggered his delusional beliefs that his wife was having an affair. At the least prospect of abandonment, no matter how tenuous, he would start to sweat, his heart rate would accelerate, and he would feel a pulse so strong, it distended the veins in his neck "like a fire hose." This arousal would throw him into alarm and panic. Thoughts about Carol having sex with a mystery man would bombard him. As he would ruminate on these, his arousal and anger would spiral upward, propelled by the imagined threat.

In group one evening, Robert revealed just how his ruminations escalated to an explosive point. Carol had been one hour late returning from a night class. As he waited for her, his "bitch tape" began to roll: "What the hell is going on here? That fucking class was over at 9:00. She should have been here by 9:30. I'll bet she's flirting with her professor!" He began to obsess on this theme. With each replay, it became a little worse. By the third replay, his wife and the professor were having sex. She was tried and convicted in the court of his mind. And, in this court, she had no defense lawyer.

In a vicious cycle, rumination heightens the internal tension. And so, as the perpetrator ruminates, he spirals upward emotionally to a state of rage. He begins to intensify whatever form of abuse is habitual for him: possessive smothering, verbal harangues, or threats of physical brutality. He becomes hypervigilant for signs of defiance. Since he projects so much of his own anger onto others, he may perceive it even where it doesn't exist.

If unchecked, rumination and escalation can go on for months until a triggering event, such as an imagined or real abandonment, culminates in homicide.[5] The most dangerous times for a woman are when she separates, when she seeks shelter, and when she becomes pregnant. (The husband fears the baby will replace him in his wife's affections.) More typically, however, the escalation continues until an abusive outburst clears the tension from the man's system.

THE PSYCHOLOGY OF THE ACUTE BATTERING PHASE

Abused wives often describe their husbands as having tantrums. Rage in intimate relationships appears out of proportion to what triggered the action, as though the perpetrator's very life were threatened. This type of rage usually exists when it feels as though one's identity is undermined. The abuser falls into an altered state, a dissociative state in which his mind seems to separate from his body. The men depict it as having a "red out." Witnesses (who are usually also victims) describe the man's eyes as "black and unfeeling" or "unfocused." "It was as though he was looking right through me," one woman told me.

Lenore Walker explains that it is not uncommon for a batterer, much like Robert, to wake his victim from a deep sleep to begin the assault. (I suspect that's because his ruminations increase late at night, when he has no distractions.) He immediately puts her into a double bind. If she answers his verbal harangue, he becomes angrier with what she says. If she is quiet, her withdrawal enrages him.

Battered women report that once the physical assault begins, only the men can stop it. All societies teach individualized responsibility for control of violence. But when aversive arousal states become high, consciousness alters, and social restraints lower, a building spiral of aggression can take over.

Social psychologist Phil Zimbardo calls this behavior "deindividuated violence" and explains it is solely under the control of the person who acts out the rage.[6] In his study of out-of-control beatings and lootings, Zimbardo outlined the breakdown of ordinary constraints that precede deindividuated violence. A person caught in its grip is unresponsive to cues from his victim. He is driven strictly from within. The physical action is even pleasurable. For the cyclical abuser, it releases the pent-up tension and rage of aversive arousal. The process feeds on itself, leading to faster and harder blows until the weapon is empty or destroyed or the abuser is exhausted.

The repeat abuser becomes addicted to this tension release. It's the only way he knows to rid himself of his bad feelings.

Zimbardo also found that anonymity increases the likelihood of deindividuated violence. What would make abusive husbands more anonymous? Perhaps there is a sense of anonymity within one's home. Certainly one is hidden from public scrutiny there.

Family violence always takes place behind closed doors. The abuser may feel he can act with impunity. As O. J. Simpson said to the police who intervened after Nicole's New Year's complaint, the issue was none of their business. It was a "family matter."

Psychologist Roy Baumeister's research on suicide notes can also help us understand the violent phase of abuse. Baumeister had analyzed the notes to discern linguistic clues that might illuminate the writer's thought processes. He found a certain tunnel vision occurs just before the suicide. He calls this "deconstructed thinking."[7] Here, an individual focuses on concrete acts and has no sense of an extended future. It's like driving in a blinding snowstorm with dim headlights. You attend only to steering and the little you can see immediately in front of you.

I believe this tunnel vision occurs just prior to abuse outbursts as well.[8] In murder-suicides, for example, the victim and perpetrator have typically been in a long-term relationship with repeated discord and battering, separations because of the abuse, and reunions. The perpetrator also has a history of depressions and substance abuse. Morbid jealousy is the central feature of his personality. His depression worsens with an apparent final breakup, and this perception triggers the violence.[9]

From reconstructing the lives of murder-suicides and from interviewing men who completed the first act but failed at the second, we see the building tension carries with it an obsessional rumination on the "problem" of the other person. The wish to destroy her becomes overwhelming. Long-term considerations such as how she might feel or the effects on the relationship cease to exist. The thought that repeats is simply: "She can't leave me, I'll show her," or "If I can't have her, nobody will."

These actions, of course, are extreme and relatively rare, but a similar process of rumination and tension buildup also appears to occur for less lethal abuse episodes. The symbolism of loss or impending loss creates extreme anxiety, rage, and tunnel vision. In this state, the perpetrator ruminates consistently on his wife's malevolence, driving the arousal and fury even higher. When he finally explodes, his rage is uncontrollable. He wants to annihilate his victim, and he will at least terrify and humiliate her. Indeed, Faye Resnick reports in her book that O. J.'s beatings were sometimes accompanied by throwing Nicole out of the house or hotel rooms semiclad. Resnick says that on one occasion, he beat her, locked her in a closet, opened the closet door, beat her again, and left her inside.

THE PSYCHOLOGY OF THE CONTRITION PHASE AND BEYOND

The contrition phase begins once the violence erupts and the tension is dispelled. This stage may involve a range of behavior, from the abuser's flat denial of what has happened, to attempts to atone, to promises of reform.

As I explained earlier, abusers may mentally reconstruct the act in order to blame the victim for having provoked the aggression. Men in treatment groups regularly begin their group participation, and literally introduce themselves, by listing their grievances against their wives. Like alcoholics who haven't confronted their addiction, these men are in denial, minimizing the severity and frequency of their violence and their responsibility for it.

If, on the other hand, the abuser is seeking atonement, his victim describes him as infantile at this stage, like a little boy caught with his hand in the cookie jar. He convinces himself and others that the battering will stop. He promises to give up alcohol, other women, or whatever his wife wants. Some men even nibble at the possibility of therapy. Visits to the hospitalized victim are accompanied by flowers, gifts, cards, and pleas for forgiveness.

Often the cyclical abuser enlists others (including the children) to plead his case. He works on his wife's guilt, and presents her as his only hope. Without her, he would be destroyed. Suicide threats are common at this time, and some may be genuine. The traditional notion that two people who love each other can surmount overwhelming odds begins to prevail. He begins to convince her, "It's you and me against the world."

The victim chooses to believe that the behavior she sees during the contrition phase indicates her husband's true nature. It hooks her on the potential of the relationship and appeals to her need to rescue him. Some wives come to me saying, "I don't want to lose this guy. I don't want to end the relationship. He's really sweet when he's not violent. Just make him stop hitting me."

Meanwhile, the man throws himself on his wife's mercy. Temporarily, she has all the power. He arouses her optimism and her sense of nurturance. She becomes acutely aware of his vulnerability: his desperation, loneliness, and alienation from any other meaningful close human contact. Threats and bribes are also common. He is bent on getting back in his wife's good graces at all costs.

These revelations often serve as added incentives to keep the woman in the relationship. Codependence evolves from them. The two partners try to convince each other and themselves that they can battle the world, that their "love" will triumph. Socialization and religious convictions also contribute. The former teaches the woman that keeping the family together is her duty, and some religions may reinforce the belief that suffering is the path to salvation. Both of these forces may suggest that a good woman will stand by her man.

The man may beg his wife to think of his career, of the family. He gets her to drop the charges and tell her friends that the black eye was an accident.

I discovered too late that Robert and Carol's rather unusual wedding occurred during the contrition phase. She was hospitalized on the day of their wedding—from injuries sustained at his hands. They had been fighting about commitment, and Robert wanted to prove how he was a changed man. He checked her out of the hospital, covered the bruises with heavy makeup, and got her in front of a wedding commissioner in three hours flat.

The contrition phase doesn't last forever, however. It fades as the man once more begins to feel anxious and vulnerable, and the next violent episode takes shape.

Two months into treatment, Robert phoned me in a panic. He said he was about to kill her. He had returned from an out-of-town business trip to find a key with a man's name on it. He "knew" his wife was having an affair, and he became enraged. Fortunately, he had learned enough to recognize imminent high risk situations for his rage.

When he came to see me, Robert was shaking and distracted. I asked to see the evidence; he showed me the key. I immediately recognized the name on it—not the name of a man but of the largest key manufacturer in town. I told him this, but he didn't believe me. I got the Yellow Pages and showed him. He appeared to calm. I asked him if he could see how he had jumped to conclusions about Carol's imagined infidelity. He agreed, but he seemed distant, distracted, as if some inner voice was competing successfully for his attention.

I spent another hour soothing Robert. I convinced him to do some deep relaxation exercises, to promise he wouldn't go home until he was completely in control. I suggested that he spend the night with a male friend. He thought that was a good idea.

Robert left and drove directly to his house and his wife. A shouting match ensued but no violence, except that he smashed into a wall while screeching out of the driveway. He then went to the friend's house. It took him three days to settle down completely. (Now I always call the woman to warn her in these situations, no matter how calm the man seems to be.)

After this, Robert was in a major crisis. Finally, Carol had had enough and left him. Suddenly, the man who was reluctant to get involved in a treatment group wanted even more therapy. He phoned me for the names of other psychologists. He needed a quick fix to get his wife back.

"She's left me. I've got a huge problem," he sobbed. "And I'm going to hurt everyone who ever gets close to me. Help me before I really hurt somebody." He called me three times a day for three weeks. In group, he took up most of the time pouring out his fear and shame. His motivation to change had suddenly gone into orbit.

Carol returned after a three-week separation. He tried to be nonchalant about it, although I knew from talking to her that he had been phoning her six times a day, sending flowers, promising to change, pointing out how much therapy he was getting, telling her that he really needed her and that, if she really loved him, she'd stand by him. He also threatened suicide if she didn't come home.

After a few weeks of feeling more secure with Carol back in the house, Robert's desperation to change began to fade. Strange signs developed. At first, it was simply a matter of relaxing his commitment to therapy. He hadn't followed up on the referrals I had made. He missed two appointments with one therapist, who then dropped him as a potential client. The rest, he never even called. He failed to show for group after he had disclosed some painful memories the previous week. When I tracked him down, he said he was getting overwhelmed and overloaded by the feelings surfacing during group.

An undercurrent started to sweep him back toward his old way of seeing things. Then he started to talk of his wife disparagingly again. Once more, I could see that he was rebuilding his ego at her expense. When he had stopped, he had felt himself on the brink of disintegration. Now, he needed to put her down to keep his fragile sense of self intact. And so the cycle of violence began anew.

■ The Woman's Experience

During the build-up phase, the victim knows all too well where the verbal attacks are leading. She can see the dark side coming. As the tension grows, the gradual descent into hell begins, paved with sarcasm, put-downs, insults, and aspersions about her abilities as a mother, a housekeeper, and a lover. Who was she calling? Who was she dressing up for? Where was she at 4:00 P.M. yesterday when he called and no one answered?

The woman, in a desperate attempt to avoid the inevitable, usually goes into a survival mode. She swallows her own outrage and caters to her man's every whim. She tries, at first, to avoid the inevitable by pacifying him, making sure nothing upsets him, doing little extra favors. It's hopeless. The fists fly, or an abrupt backhander sends her reeling. And, sometimes, sensing that it is unavoidable, she may even provoke him, just to get it over with. She comes to learn that the violence builds inside him, like water accumulating behind a dam—a dam that is destined to burst.

During an assault, the victim quickly realizes that escape is futile. She usually dissociates. Women describe leaving their bodies with their mind. A surrealistic state of calm may occur during which the wife experiences the abuse like a slow-motion movie. This may be coupled with a sense of disbelief, as with Carla, a sense that the incident is not really happening to her.

After the violence, the victim's reactions are similar to those who have experienced a natural disaster. These typically involve emotional collapse within twenty-two to forty-eight hours after the catastrophe and symptoms of post-traumatic stress such as listlessness, depression, and feelings of helplessness. Victims tend to isolate themselves for some time, in an attempt to heal and to avoid the shame that accompanies having their injuries detected by friends.

■The Role of Alcohol

Frequently, battering occurs when assaultive men are inebriated, and they often blame the violence on alcohol. Even Denise Brown's description of O. J. Simpson throwing Nicole out of the house was prefaced by her admission that they had spent the evening at a Mexican restaurant, drinking tequila.

In order to find out what role drugs and alcohol play in the cycle of violence, my research partner and I screened abusive men for substance abuse.[10] We found that assaultive men, in general, have very high alcohol use scores. Indeed, the more a man matched our gauge for having an abusive personality, the greater his alcohol consumption.

Men who have this profile also experience depression and anxiety—so-called *dysphoric* states. Alcohol is one of the common ways they learn to suppress and blot out these uncomfortable feelings. So is anger. Unfortunately, since these individuals experience the dysphoric feelings as a function of their personalities, and since alcohol is a disinhibitor—that is, it relaxes one's inhibitions—what results is a volatile combination of unhappy, angry men who have lost all restraint. This puts them at an ever greater risk for violence. Alcohol and anger clear out depression but unfortunately, they do so at great cost to the drinker.

It is a mistake, however, to blame alcohol for the violence. As I point out to the men in my treatment groups, a lot of people get drunk and don't punch their wives. Some try to give their money away or sing in the shower. Others wind up with lampshades on their heads or fast asleep.

Whatever actions emerge when a disinhibitor enters the picture are a part of a person's learned repertoire. When people say, "The alcohol made me do it," they're blaming one symptom—violence—on another—alcohol. These are both aspects of an abusive personality.

So while there is an association between alcohol use and violence, one does not cause the other. Both are traced back to an earlier aspect of the self. One's personality is formed much sooner than one learns to use alcohol or to hit.

■ The Dance of Traumatic Bonding

Janet came to see me as a private client with an unusual problem. She was about forty-five, attractive, a little overweight. She was a lawyer who specialized, ironically, in defending wife assaulters in court. She was aware of a little-known loophole, resulting in the man having abusive incidents expunged from his record.

She had met Dave, a man fifteen years her junior, and had established an intense relationship with him. He was very abusive. Once he forced her through a game of Russian roulette, putting the gun barrel in her mouth and clicking its hammer on two empty chambers. Another time he feigned suicide, firing a shot in the closet.

She attempted to escape to a local battered women's center, but when it was discovered what she had been doing for a living, she was less than popular. When she first came to see me, she seemed focused and businesslike. She explained how her boyfriend told her she was getting "old and ugly," and how he slapped her and pushed her in a closet.

"How can I get away from him?" she asked.

I told her about changing her locks, installing security systems, carrying a cell phone, and calling 911. She looked blank. There was a sense of helplessness about her, yet I knew she was a highly professional trial lawyer.

I made an appointment to see her the following week. She canceled and rebooked. Then, she canceled and rebooked again. When she finally came in, two weeks later, her first question was, "Why did I say I wanted to leave Dave? I can't remember."

I read back to her my case notes from her first session; she looked shocked and saddened. I could tell that the undertow had begun. When I saw her three weeks later, she looked disheveled and distracted, as if she were coming off a drinking binge. "Tell me again," she said, "why I should leave this guy."

It is often asked why women stay in such damaging relationships. For some, as suggested above, the sweetness and power of the contrition phase (some call it the "honeymoon" stage) are overwhelmingly seductive. These women unconsciously collude with their abusers in denial. Others become so beaten down that they seem to lose all will to care for themselves.

In 1988 another sensational abuse story hit the press that seemed to describe new depths of horror. Hedda Nussbaum was arrested along with her lover, Joel Steinberg, for the murder of their six-year-old adopted daughter, Lisa.[11] When Nussbaum took the stand in a New York courtroom in December 1988, the spectators and millions who watched on television were mesmerized by her chilling story of drug abuse, systematic beatings, and a life of squalor behind a middle-class façade.

Nussbaum's story was one of her total devotion to a man who stripped her of all human dignity. Her first day of testimony ended with the image of a helpless child laying comatose on a bathroom floor while her parents ignored her and freebased cocaine. Nussbaum might have saved her daughter with a phone call, but didn't for fear of angering the man she loved, the man who had left her with a fighter's face: a flattened nose, a distorted eye, and a cleft lip.

Prosecutors agreed with medical testimony that Nussbaum was a psychological slave, incapable of the ability or the will to save her daughter. They dropped all charges against her.

This strange loyalty has been likened to the paradoxical bonds that form between hostages and victims in what is sometimes referred to as the Stockholm syndrome (so called because a bank teller in Stockholm, Sweden, reportedly fell in love with the man who had held her captive).[12] Anna Freud coined the term *identification with the aggressor* to describe this process.[13] When someone is in a life-and-death situation in which she is powerless against a potentially lethal other, she comes to identify with that person as a means of warding off danger. According to Anna Freud, a potential victim believes that if she could see the world through the eyes of the aggressor, she might be able to save herself from destruction.

Bruno Bettelheim described how this process worked in a Nazi prison camp with inmates who emulated their captors in a last ditch attempt to prevent indiscriminate punishment.[14] The psychological key here is that the injury was severe and *random*. People will do anything to try make random danger controllable. One strategy is to imagine the world through the eyes of those in power. It's a desperate act, but so is the situation.

Susan Painter and I have written several papers in which we suggest that something akin to this occurs to battered women. We call this *traumatic bonding* and argue that it is based on two aspects of an abusive relationship: one person holding more power than the other and intermittent abuse.[15] Unpredictability is also key: Intermittent reinforcement is a powerful motivator that keeps one coming back for more (take, for example, the lure of slot machines). The victim's hope is that maybe this time it will be better; maybe this time, he'll stop. And for reasons she cannot understand, powerful emotional bonds keep pulling her back—bonds forged by intermittent reinforcement.

There is no special deficit in a battered woman's personality that makes her susceptible to getting trapped in an abusive relationship. To the contrary, the features of the relationship itself are sufficient to account for the trapping.

The bonds that bind abuse victims to their tormenters are legendary. They are like giant bungee cords. As the woman dives out of the relationship, the cords stretch to the breaking point. But the further she gets, the greater the tension to snap back. The need for homeostasis maintains the status quo of the system. As the days pass, the bad memories fade, and only the good ones remain, fed by the woman's desire to sate her man's neediness, a neediness that only builds until the next incident.

PART II

The Creation of a Cyclical Batterer

4 Post-Traumatic Stress Disorder: A Telling Clue

THE MORE I WORKED WITH MEN WHO INTERMITTENTLY ASSAULTED their intimate partners, the more I wanted to understand what motivated their behavior and fueled their emotions. What caused them to alternately lash out and become contrite? Why only with their wives? Why only in private? Why the excessive jealousy and rage?

I am not the only one to have posed these questions about intimate violence. Over the years, many theories have been advanced to answer them. Each viewed intimate abuse through its own lens, but none gave the full story.

The Brain Damage Theory

Experts have divided aggression into two categories: "normal," which is directed toward an enemy, and "abnormal," which is directed toward a stranger or a loved one—the act of a madman.

Like Dr. Frankenstein's cursed monster who was implanted with a "criminal" brain, medical science believed that wife assaulters committed violence because of an aberration in the brain structure. At a 1977 international forensic psychiatry conference I attended, for example, all the research papers on wife assault focused exclusively on its neurological causes.

Frank Elliott, a psychiatrist at the Pennsylvania Hospital, one of the leading proponents of this theory, believed that occurrences of explosive rage, or *episodic dyscontrol*, were caused by an electronic microstorm in the limbic system, the "ancient" part of the brain situated in the brainstem that is believed to be the seat of emotion.[1]

He described dyscontrol as periods of intense rage "triggered by trivial irritations and accompanied by verbal or physical violence." The individual usually has a "warm, pleasant personality," but may have "a history of traffic accidents resulting from aggressive driving."[2]

According to Elliott, the most common "organic" condition associated with intimate violence is temporal lobe epilepsy (an uncontrolled electrical discharge in the area of the brain that regulates strong emotions). This condition, in turn, could have been caused by any early trauma to the brain such as an interruption to the oxygen supply during birth or infancy or other traumatic scars. Elliott did not speculate as to how these scars might have occurred. He also did not explicitly connect temporal lobe epilepsy to being a victim of physical abuse, although more recent research has shown that childhood victimization is a strong risk factor for adult abusiveness in men.[3] In addition, he believed metabolic disorders such as hypoglycemia could also trigger intimate rage.

Elliott provided a literary example that unintentionally demonstrates the shortcomings of the concept of episodic dyscontrol. He cites Emile Zola's character Jacque in *La Bete Humaine* whom he describes as "a man with the symptoms of temporal lobe epilepsy who could not always control an urge to kill women who attracted him."[4] (I have to wonder how a neurological disorder leads one to attack *only* desirable women.)

More recent psychiatric explanations have maintained this focus. One published in 1989 found that 61 percent of men assessed for outpatient treatment for wife assault had received prior head injuries.[5]

In another study, a group of fifteen men (out of 443 studied) were diagnosed with intermittent explosive disorder (IED), an "organic" impulse control condition closely related to episodic dyscontrol. An individual with IED is not psychotic or aggressive between episodes, but bursts intermittently into an uncontrollable rage out of all proportion to what preceded it. Ironically, these researchers failed to recognize the significance of their findings: The typical victim of the outbursts was "a spouse, lover, or boyfriend/girlfriend."[6]

In all honesty, I must add that some men who come to my treatment groups do have the obvious "soft signs" of neurological disorder, which include pronounced *nystagmus* (jerky eye movements) and attention deficits. Mark was such a client. He had these symptoms as well as an IQ level in the dull-normal range.

Mark was a huge, beefy man with the reflective capacity of an eight-year-old. He had had a horrible, conflicted relationship with his mother and was now living with Maggie, a woman twenty years his senior, who was also his boss. My cotherapist and I didn't like his chances for success, but we decided we had to try something because he wasn't going to receive therapy anywhere else.

Mark gave Maggie a black eye within a few weeks of starting treatment. When I asked him if he knew when he was getting angry, he said, "Yes." When I inquired why he didn't take a time out to calm down, he looked dumbfounded, as if I had demanded that he explain Einstein's theory of relativity. It was clear he was only taking in limited information and that his deficits were more than we could handle in the treatment group. I have seen other men who I also believed had neurological damage. But in every case, they too had had rageful relationships with their parents. The neurology, by itself, was only part of the story.

Indeed, in study after study, neurological explanations for abuse seem to avoid the obvious: that something about the intimate relationships generates the violence. If it only occurs in the context of intimacy and typically in private, how then is it "uncontrollable"?

Let's again consider Robert. Although he may have felt some vague discomfort the night of his wife's office party, he didn't act aggressively while there or even express his uneasiness to his wife. Although his beliefs about Carol's affair were delusional, he was not in any other way psychotic. He didn't hallucinate that the sky was opening and a giant eye was watching him. He was in touch with reality as others experience it. He was entirely capable of carrying out his job as a deep-sea diver—surely a dangerous occupation for a psychotic. Also, Robert was not a psychopath. He deeply regretted what he had done and had even called the police himself the night he assaulted Carol.

And what about Meyer? He too was responsible and likable between bouts of violence. But his rage states would come on suddenly, usually after a brief period of withdrawal. They involved his talking himself into a frenzy about how hard he worked, how unappreciated he was, and how much of his money Carol spent. Meyer was not psychotic and probably not psychopathic. Would a psychiatrist label him as suffering from intermittent explosive disorder? He did, after all, meet the diagnostic criteria.

But if he did suffer from IED how was he, too, able to explode only in private places or when no one else was around? And perhaps more significantly, how did he snap into a calm, controlling mode when the police arrived? He was even capable of restraining himself when his son entered the room and yelled at him to "stop hitting Mommy."

Intimate violence is a complex action, filled with rich symbolism of the woman as lover/savior/mother/betrayer. It is awash with obsessions and revulsions, tensions, jealousy, and rage. How can one reduce it to a simple perturbation in the limbic system? How does scar tissue lead one to attack only one's wife and only in private? Clearly, some higher order of mental association that relates the victim to the perpetrator and the context of the violence must direct and influence the assault.

We must ask ourselves, what does the man's wife mean to him? What symbolic baggage does he carry from his earlier days that gives shape to this meaning? What is it about intimacy that alters his view of the other person? Why, for example, would the rage not be generalized to whoever else is nearby?

Episodic dyscontrol or intermittent explosive disorder would lead us to expect random times for attacks that could occur just as easily in public as in private. But the research on wife assault suggest this is not at all a haphazard act. Something more is going on. Something that guides the focus of rage, something learned about male-female relationships. Something that is not organic.

■The Genetic Mandate

In the 1970s, another way of understanding human aggression, sociobiology, became popular. This discipline studies how human social behaviors may be genetically encoded and are inherited through a process of natural selection. Spurred by the influential work of E. O. Wilson, a biologist at Harvard University, sociobiology began to influence thinking about behavior in general, and wife assault in particular.[7]

Sociobiologists see abuse as a man's way to dominate an intimate female in order to guarantee reproductive and sexual exclusivity. In their view, a man hits his intimate partner in order to satisfy the biological imperative that his genes be passed along to the next generation.

In his book *The Evolution of Desire*, David Buss, one of sociobiology's leading adherents, argues that this strategy is hardwired into our genes and makes evolutionary sense. Since fertilization occurs internally within the female, the way for a male to maximize his contribution to the gene pool is to have sex with as many women as possible while maintaining exclusive sexual access—in effect, to keep a harem. But females, who have the private responsibility for bearing and nurturing the child, improve their odds of successful reproduction by choosing a mate who has access to resources and is inclined to make these resources available to her *alone*.

These strategies are at loggerheads. Men cannot fulfill their short-term wishes without interfering with women's long-term goals and vice versa. Buss argues that emotions such as anger and jealousy are signals that male and female reproductive strategies are in conflict.

Insults about the woman's appearance are a man's way of securing "a more favorable power balance within the relationship."[8] The sexual content of swearing at a woman (by calling her the cultural expletives for a loose woman) embarrasses her into submission. The insults guarantee sexual exclusivity. As Buss puts it, "Women are more often the victims and men are more often the perpetrators of condescension and other forms of psychological abuse. . . . Victims often feel that, because their mating alternatives are not rosy, they must strive valiantly to placate the current mate. . . . Men's motives for physically battering women center heavily on coercive control."[9]

According to this view, the disproportionate male jealousy that accompanies abuse stems from a man's uncertainty about his contribution to the gene pool—something that is assured for women. This male doubt underlies the higher rates of violence and even homicide based on jealousy. Abandonment, in the eyes of a sociobiologist, is an opportunity to procreate seen slipping away.

The logic of sociobiology raises many questions. Is violence toward an intimate partner the product of a million years of evolution? If it is part of "human nature," why aren't all men assaultive? Are men who punch and kick their wives simply playing out a sociobiological mandate handed down through natural selection? If it is inevitable, why should we punish individual transgressors? Would it be possible to stop the violence through short-term treatment? Could we stop in sixteen weeks what took hundreds of thousands of years to develop? The implications are staggering.

And, if sexual threat is so great for males, why don't more of them attack the interlopers? This occurs with much less frequency than violence directed toward wives. And why is attacking one's wife the evolutionarily sound response? If a woman is pregnant, and another male is going to raise the child, why not move on and impregnate someone else?

Also, why are the rates so high for physical violence directed toward pregnant women? That makes no sense from a sociobiological perspective. Why would a man bent on passing along his genes endanger his progeny and the source of future descendants? Yet researchers have found that 58 percent of women reporting some form of violent victimization were pregnant when the abuse began.[10]

While the neurological view is too narrow, the sociobiological explanation for abuse is so broad that it too fails to take into account another obvious fact: that only a small percentage of men physically assault their wives.

■ Male Tyranny: The Feminist View

In her book *Conjugal Crime*, Terry Davidson describes the long social history of wife abuse.[11] It stretches back as far as the eye can see. From the Old Testament advocacy of stoning any woman who could not prove her virginity to the church exhorting men to uphold their divine responsibility to beat their wives, organized religion and the law have sanctioned abuse toward women.

Consider Gratian's *Decretum,* a twelfth-century religious tract and systemization of church law that held, "Women should be subject to their men. . . . Woman is not made of God's image. . . . Woman's authority is nil. . . . Adam was beguiled by Eve . . . not she by him. It is right that he whom woman led into wrongdoing should have her under his direction so that he may not fall a second time through female levity."[12]

This view of woman guided Christian ethics and laws throughout the Middle Ages, including the infamous Inquisition and the witch trials in Europe that saw 300,000 women burned at the stake. Fra Cherubino's *Rules of Marriage*, written in the fifteenth century and serving as a marriage guide for the Catholic church for four hundred years, exhorted a husband to "scold her sharply, bully and terrify her. And if that still doesn't work, take up a stick and beat her soundly, for it is better to punish the body and correct the soul than to damage the soul and spare the body."[13]

Davidson believes that men, threatened by the mystery of women's inexplicable ability to create life, found sociolegal means of quashing that terrible force. This subjugation included the invention of exclusively female evil attributes that justified repression. In the Middle Ages, these encompassed a susceptibility to the influences of the devil (described in detail in Jacob Sprenger's *Malleus Maleficarum*[14]) and, in modern times, "penis envy," Freud's conviction that women, in general, suffer from feelings of inferiority to the male possession of a penis.

Lest we believe these attitudes are a thing of the past, Davidson quotes actor Oliver Reed as saying in 1976, "basically the only way to make a woman feel secure is to give her enough of the old oats. . . . Yes, I've smacked a couple of women in the past. . . . You put her across your knee and give her one." And Aristotle Onassis said to a woman he had beaten to the point of exhaustion, "All Greek men, without exception, beat their wives. It's good for them."[15]

Based on this long history of abuse toward women, daily experiences in battered women's shelters, and the emergent feminist academic scholarship, a new theory explaining wife assault arose in the 1970s. The feminist perspective focused on the role of patriarchy and male domination to answer the question, Why do men beat their wives?

To feminists, a man batters because he expects to have all the power and be the boss. These expectations develop from the way boys are raised in our culture—their male sex role identification—which prepares them for "male privilege." Men have been socialized to dominate. They learn to exercise this privilege through violence. What's more, this control is always directed outward. They are woefully inept at monitoring what is within, emotions such as anger or jealousy.

Wife assault, therefore, is "normal" violence committed not by madmen but by those who believe that patriarchy is their right, that marriage gives them unrestricted control over their wives, and that hitting is an acceptable means of establishing this control. Indeed, violence preserves the status quo, with men at the top of the power hierarchy. As researchers Russell Dobash and Emerson Dobash put it, "Men who assault their wives are actually living up to cultural prescriptions that are cherished in Western society—aggressiveness, male dominance, and female subordination—and they are using physical force as a means to enforce that dominance."[16]

The feminist view focuses on society rather than individuals as the cause of male abusiveness: Domination of women is a cultural prescription, and violence against them a means to that end. This emphasis on the cultural is reflected in the feminist distrust of psychological causes of male violence.[17]

In fact, much feminist analysis argues that it is misguided to emphasize psychopathology to explain wife assault because violence results from "normal psychological and behavioral patterns of most men."[18] All too often, we use a damaging childhood or drug abuse to exonerate an individual perpetrator, simultaneously absolving him of his crimes and precluding a hard look at the society that fostered his behavior.

This analysis shone a light into the abandoned social context of male abusiveness and found the power, domination, and male privilege that male psychiatrists had conveniently overlooked. Feminists were also uncomfortable with sociobiology, which made male jealousy, domination, abuse, and philandering sound like some inevitable biological blueprint.

Eventually though, research data began to accumulate that called for a more complex view of wife assault. All available evidence indicated that men who had been similarly socialized showed great variation when it came to their behavior toward women. An assortment of large, sophisticated sample surveys of women conducted in the United States and Canada between 1975 and 1992 disclosed that in any given year, about 89 percent of male partners were not violent. Only 3 or 4 percent committed injurious acts, such as punching or kicking, and of these men, only two-thirds repeated the violence.[19]

When female interviewers asked women to complete a survey on conflict in the family, more than 70 percent reported their husbands were nonviolent throughout the marriage. Were these men just asserting domination in another way? Not really. Only about 9 percent reported their husbands to be domineering.

Just as considerable variation exists in male behavior, it also exists in family power arrangements. Again, research studies found great diversity here. In one such investigation at the University of New Hampshire, Diane Coleman and Murray Straus assessed marital power by asking "Who has the final say?" in decisions about buying a car, having children, the choice of house or apartment, jobs, and the weekly food budget. In less than 10 percent of the couples the man was dominant, and in about 7 percent the woman was. The rest described their marriages as divided power (54 percent) or egalitarian (29 percent).[20] These results seemed to indicate that a variety of power arrangements exist and that male dominance is more rare than feminists believe.

Moreover, research on gay and lesbian abuse rates allows us to separate intimacy from gender. When we do this, we find that no matter how people couple, abusiveness persists. Lesbians, for example, are even more violent than heterosexuals in intimate relationships.[21] And my recent research with gay males shows the same psychological factors that predict abusiveness in heterosexual couples applies as well to gay couples.[22]

All of these research findings seem to indicate that the impact of socialization on individual men varies greatly. Men hold widely dissimilar beliefs about women, have diverse individual levels of personal power with them, and act in varied ways toward them. The abusive-domineering male "created" by socialization and historical forces is, in fact, in the minority. The broad-based feminist theory makes such global statements that it fails to explain these individual variations in actions occurring in intimate relationships.

■ Social Learning Theory

Recently, the television news program *48 Hours* reported the case of Lonnie Dutton (no relation, I assure you), an Oklahoma man who had physically, emotionally, and sexually abused his children for years. Among other things, he kicked his twelve- and fifteen-year-old sons with steel-toed boots, ordered them to throw darts at their ten-year-old sister, and beat them if they didn't steal enough groceries from the market.[23] Finally, the boys banded together and shot him to death. After they were found guilty, the community rallied to free them. A judge has deferred their sentencing until 1996.

As is usual in these cases, people who knew this man came forward to say that in public, at least, he was a nice guy. As one buddy explained, "You always knew where you stood with Lonnie." The show also recounted that Lonnie had himself been the victim of physical abuse at the hands of his father. A medical doctor explained that Lonnie was violent because he had had a violent role model. This doctor's explanation is the social learning view in a nutshell.

In 1963, a small group of nursery school children took part in an experiment that led to the development of social learning theory. Depending on the group to which they had been assigned, the preschoolers watched an adult aggressively attack an inflatable "Bobo doll," watched a film of an adult doing the same, watched a cartoon with an aggressive character, or experienced no exposure to aggression at all. Soon after, the children were mildly frustrated when the experimenter took away a favorite toy. Those youngsters who had had previous exposure to aggression behaved more belligerently than those who did not.[24]

In follow-up studies, the original investigator, Albert Bandura, found that high-status adults (such as parents) are the most effective models for aggression, and dependent children are the most compliant learners. Punishing a child for acting aggressively inhibits those displays only in the parent's presence. The behavior goes underground, surfacing when the punitive parent is absent. The fathers of aggressive adolescent boys punished them severely for their behavior. Paradoxically, these parents produced the very activity they were trying to stamp out.[25]

Social learning theory examines how habitual actions, such as violence, are acquired through observation of others, and how these are maintained by social payoffs called *rewards*. (The reward can originate with one's own body. Large muscular children may learn that they can resolve conflicts through aggression; because of their stature, they're more likely to be rewarded for physical actions, including violence, although not all large children become violent.) These theorists examine individuals' unique learning experiences to discover opportunities the subjects might have had to observe actions they would eventually perform.

From this perspective, wife assaulters are believed to copy, or *model*, violence they observed in their families of origin. Research has shown that watching their fathers hit their mothers did make men more likely to assault their wives.[26] Furthermore, there are built-in instant rewards for battering: Men "win" arguments that may have been going badly. Faced with what they believe are their wives' superior verbal and emotional skills, they fall back on their one advantage: physical superiority. They feel *agentic*; that is, they act out and control the situation the way they think real men are supposed to.

Social learning theory has advantages over the other explanations of wife assault: It accounts for individual variations in behavior, and it relates wife assault to a large body of general studies on aggression.

However, there are still problems. For one thing, according to this theory, violence is always triggered by an external event. Like a rat in a maze, the wife assaulter reacts to the external trigger. But partners of assaultive men typically report that the men themselves generate tension. They become irritable for no apparent reason. Rather than passively responding to incidents in their environment, these men inevitably and repeatedly create the event that triggers their violence.

In addition, observational learning doesn't lead to violence in the linear fashion that this theory predicts. Aggression by either parent toward the other can increase violence and victimization by sons and daughters. In other cases, as in my own father's, the witness of interparental abuse defines himself in opposition to his model. He does everything he can to avoid becoming like the violent parent.

Something more complex than mere copying of actions is going on. Abusive men experience profound depressions, delusional jealousy, and disproportionate rage—all in an intimate context. How does one model the inner experience of depression? A deeper, more pervasive form of personality disturbance seems to be at wo.rk than what social learning theory would describe.

■A Telling Clue

None of these theories answered all my questions about cyclical abusers, and some raised new ones. I was dissatisfied, and decided to pursue my own research into the origins of their personalities. I covered many areas, as you will see in the following chapters. But after I had engaged in this study for some time, I stumbled upon a feature I had not expected. And this clue indicated not a physiological, genetic, societal, or socially learned theory but rather a psychological basis for abuse that originated in early development.

The clue to an earlier origin was that cyclically assaultive men experienced the symptoms of post-traumatic stress disorder (PTSD), the normal reaction anyone would have to a highly disturbing situation such as an attack or natural disaster. PTSD symptoms include depression (crying, sadness, feelings of inferiority), anxiety (tension, trouble breathing, panic attacks), sleep disturbance (restlessness, nightmares, early morning awakenings), and dissociation (spacing out, flashbacks, dizziness, out of body experiences).

My client Mike's experience was typical. This twenty-eight-year-old came into the group looking like a fugitive from a punk rock band; he was clad in black leather and adorned with earrings, a nose ring, and various other body piercings. His head was shaved clean.

Mike was extremely quiet during the first group meeting—hardly uttering a word. Afterward, he tentatively approached me. "Being in here with these other men makes me so anxious," he said softly, "I don't know what to do. I'm afraid. I don't want to be here. I can't talk."

Despite his docile demeanor, I knew Mike had been convicted of hitting his girlfriend. So I calmed him, suggesting he take it one week at a time.

For the first five or six sessions, Mike continued to be withdrawn. He struggled to stay in the group. By the seventh session he began to warm up. "I have these nightmares," he said. "Something scary is coming after me, but I can't make out what it is. I wake up in a sweat. And afterward, I can't sleep for the rest of the night." He also admitted to feeling depressed and suicidal. He wanted to hurt himself. He was living in a halfway house, recovering from an addiction to heroin.

Once, when I asked Mike if he had had any dissociative experiences—that is, if he felt things weren't real, as if he were watching himself in a movie—he brightened and said, "Yeah! That's it."

The batterers whom I researched scored high on tests used to measure trauma symptoms such as those Mike described.[27] In fact, their psychological profiles were surprisingly similar to other groups of men, such as Vietnam veterans, who had been diagnosed with PTSD.

At first, this was confusing to me. Common sense dictates that only victims suffer trauma symptoms—not perpetrators. Were batterers also victims? Because they were abusive and aggressive, we don't usually think so. Besides, most of these men were unwilling or unable to describe their past. They had great difficulty talking about their emotions. Further analysis and study was needed.

In 1987, Harvard psychiatrist Bessel van der Kolk described how children who had been traumatized experienced rage reactions and difficulties modulating their aggression.[28] There was a link here. I had to wonder which traumas occurred regularly in the childhoods of the men I had been studying that might underlie their fury. The PTSD-like symptoms they reported and their chronic anger and abusiveness all pointed to a common early source.

In an attempt to understand the connection between early trauma and wife assault, I gave groups of assaultive and nonabusive men a questionnaire that assessed their childhood memories.[29] I wanted to know if their parents were warm or cold, accepting or rejecting. I found that those who reported cold, rejecting parents experienced more severe, extensive, and frequent trauma symptoms. I developed a different questionnaire to measure shaming actions that parents might have used against the men when they were boys. Again, those who had been shamed as children also had intense trauma symptoms.

These results suggested that chronic adult trauma symptoms and abusive behavior might originate in childhood experiences.

With further investigation, I found that they were related to painful experiences of shaming, rejection, and abusiveness in the men's upbringing.[30] Mike, for example, eventually opened the Pandora's box of his childhood, revealing that he had been severely and randomly beaten by his alcoholic father. Although abusive men can't express it verbally, they seemed to experience some early form of trauma that has numerous effects beyond just modeling abusive actions. These effects manifest themselves globally in their sense of self, their inability to trust, their delusional jealousy, their mood cycles, their view of the world. They form what I have come to call the abusive personality.

I theorized that as the adult batterer cycles through the phases of abuse, he becomes not one personality but two. Just as a woman's dissociation may help her cope with the inescapable terror of sexual abuse, so may men have learned other aspects of trauma reaction, such as emotional volatility and rage, to cope with being victimized. They may use and eventually misuse these mechanisms, as with any other trauma response, long after the original terror is gone, and when conditions no longer call for them. Now they are inappropriate, even destructive.

As I gathered research results, I could see how early experiences can have lasting effects that go far beyond the copying of violent actions. They influence every aspect of the man's "intimate personality": how he sees his wife, how he feels, how he thinks about the causes of his problems.

I found that the psychological seeds of abusiveness are sown very early in life—even during infancy. The development of the abusive personality is a gradual process that builds over years. As we will see in much greater detail in the following chapters, the seeds come from three distinct sources: being shamed, especially by one's father; an insecure attachment to one's mother; and the direct experience of abusiveness in the home. No one factor is sufficient to create the abusive personality; these elements must exist simultaneously for the personality to develop. They create a potential for abusiveness that is shaped and refined by later experiences, but that potential develops early in life.

As I delved deeper into the psychological basis for the abusive personality, a picture slowly began to emerge—a picture that gradually gained clarity and definition, as if it had been removed from a photographic bath.

⑤ Shame: The Father's Contribution

IN 1988, I WAS INVITED TO BE A DOMESTIC VIOLENCE EXPERT on the *Sally Jessy Raphaël Show*. Among the other guests was a recovered violent couple. The man had assaulted his wife for years, sought therapy, stopped his abuse, and eventually became an advocate for awareness and treatment.

To my surprise, the audience was extremely hostile toward this couple. One man, sputtering with rage, chastised the formerly abusive husband. "I don't understand guys like you," he said. "How can you do that to your wife? You come on this show and tell us that you're a good guy now, but it doesn't change the past." And an irate woman told the wife, "There must be something wrong with you to stay with a beast like that."

Instead of calmly providing information, I was thrown into the role of defending this couple for having the courage to come out publicly. I asked the audience how many of them felt they dealt with their anger constructively. Not many raised their hands.

Later, I wondered how the angry audience members handled conflicts at home. Like them, many of us have been quick to judge wife assaulters as beasts or misogynists. But I believe these judgments and the assaultive men's inability to articulate their experience have conspired to keep unexpressed the complete story of the development of abusiveness. And one of the original elements these men have the greatest difficulty exploring, but which has had the most profound impact on their anger, is their sense of shame.

■ An All Right Guy

In 1992 I was an expert witness in the trial of Ignacio, a Hispanic teenage boy who had shot and killed Oscar, his abusive stepfather. Oscar was a respected, even heroic, black police officer and a member of the Emergency Response Team and the National Guard. He was also a black belt in karate. No one, especially not Oscar's police and National Guard buddies, would believe he had been abusive, but there was strong evidence from prior 911 calls, disclosures to family friends, and corroborated stories from family members.

When I came to Ignacio's home to interview him for the upcoming trial, he was wearing an electronic ankle bracelet to monitor his location. The house was immaculate. The living room contained a shrine to the dead Oscar: his ashes, trophies, and medals, flowers, and several pictures. Ignacio's mother, Rosa, exhibiting great loyalty to her dead husband's memory, refused to talk with me about his abusiveness toward her and her children. "When the trial comes," she said, "I will speak then."

I turned to Ignacio: "Describe your stepfather to me."

"He was an all right guy, pretty good to me sometimes. We started arguing, though. He complained a lot and would scream. I think he was under a lot of pressure at work."

"How do you feel about him?"

"I'm kinda mad sometimes."

In addition to the standing harangues, it turned out that Oscar had constantly belittled Ignacio and had lashed him with a heavy leather belt. It took several interviews before we even scratched the surface of his abuse.

Oscar acted like a drill sergeant at home, inspecting the cleanliness of the house after the kids had done their chores. He seemed to have it in for the eldest. He would berate Ignacio daily, for hours on end, telling him that he was worthless and would never amount to anything. He would flick karate blows and kicks just inches from Ignacio's head, threatening to kill him, insisting that he couldn't escape. Sometimes those swipes connected: the youngster had lost hearing in one ear from having been beaten about the head.

Ignacio had to take the tirades for hours. If he so much as looked away, the punishment would escalate. Rosa was at work during most of these incidents, but when she was home, she rarely intervened. Oscar had assaulted her, too.

During these bouts, Ignacio experienced the unpleasant state of aversive arousal. He was learning that he couldn't avoid his stepfather's wrath, that he was a helpless captive of its grip. No matter how bad it made him feel, he had to stand there and take it.

Psychologist Martin Seligman experimented with dogs that he placed in a similar negative situation. He put them in harnesses so they could not escape electric shocks to their paws. When Seligman removed the harnesses and reapplied the shocks, the dogs just laid down and took them. They didn't try to escape, even when it was possible. This behavioral unresponsiveness is called *learned helplessness*.[1]

Of course, a person caught in such a loathsome situation may behave in the same way, but he has an emotional response as well. Since any expression of rage can be severely punished, the victim must swallow his feelings. This state of captivity can induce shame, since it undercuts one's sense of mastery and control of one's fate, steals human dignity, and forces one to dissociate from the horror as a means of coping.

Ignacio was learning these same lessons at Oscar's school of hard knocks. In fact, when the prosecutor at his trial asked the youth why he hadn't run away if the situation was so bad, he responded with puzzlement, "It never crossed my mind."

I knew better. When he was being subjected to abuse, Ignacio was learning that neither aggression nor escape would succeed in reducing the aversive arousal he was feeling. These responses were being scrubbed from his repertoire of reactions to his stepfather.

As the abuse intensified, Ignacio became increasingly despondent and suicidal. One night, when Oscar started in on him again, the boy ran to get his stepfather's service revolver from its storage compartment in the closet of the master bedroom. He was going to kill himself.

He darted into the backyard with the gun when Oscar intercepted him and began yelling, "What the hell are you doing? You don't move when I talk to you. If I get my hands on you—" In a confusion of terror and rage, Ignacio turned and fired several shots behind him in the dark, in his stepfather's direction. One bullet killed Oscar instantly.

Ignacio fled from his tormentor, toward the back of the yard, not realizing that he had shot him. Suspecting that Oscar was using his Emergency Response Team training and circling around him, he waited in frozen terror—the same state he had experienced in the past during Oscar's vituperations and beatings. He paced in circles and, at one point, passed out from the fear and hyperarousal. After some time had elapsed, however, he decided to approach the house cautiously. There in the alley, between the house and the garage, he saw Oscar's body. Ignacio still didn't recognize the truth. He believed his stepfather was playing dead.

Often when abuse victims fight back, as Ignacio did, they cannot fathom that their actions have any consequences on the abuser. They perceive that person as all-powerful—invincible. They have learned this from years of powerlessness.

The judge and jury took Ignacio's maltreatment into account when they sentenced him to fourteen months in a minimum-security prison for the reduced charge of second-degree manslaughter.

(Although law professor Alan Dershowitz calls this "the abuse excuse," it's not that simple. There are times, especially with trapped and battered children, where a case can be made for diminished responsibility.) Ignacio served his time, but he wasn't completely out of danger. Because of the patterns established in his childhood, he was still at great risk for becoming a wife abuser.

Ignacio's case was extreme: he killed his persecutor. But much like battered women, most abused boys cannot extricate themselves from their misfortune. Their parents have all the power. Eventually, usually by the time they reach adolescence, they run away or physically fight the abusive adult. When emotional abuse is not accompanied by violence, flight becomes less tenable. The attack is insufficient to drive the boy from the home, and in most cases, he feels he can ride out the storm, unaware of its future effects on him.

■ Finding Shame

Clearly, there is more than mere modeling going on in abusive families. My investigations into the pasts of cyclic abusers reveal that, like Ignacio, most were punished severely physically and emotionally by their fathers and in a way that would impact their later behavior toward their wives. For not only were they beaten, they were also rejected and shamed.

I compared assaultive and nonassaultive men's memories of their childhoods to assess their recollections of their parents' warmth.[2] I wanted to understand the connection between being abused as a child and becoming abusive as an adult.

In my research, I used a psychological instrument developed in Sweden, the EMBU, which translates into English as "Memories of My Upbringing." This may sound similar to Marcel Proust's great work, *Remembrance of Things Past*, but the resemblance goes beyond the title. Just as Proust was attempting to connect adult sensations to their origin, the EMBU can provide, for those of us less reflective than Proust, a look back into our childhoods. By asking questions that we may not have pondered for years, the EMBU opens up feelings and memories. These, of course, can be colored by time and current circumstances, and they do not necessarily represent exact recordings of past events, but the memories or their interpretations can be illuminating.

In using this scale, I found that the recollections of assaultive males were characterized by memories of rejecting, cold, and abusive fathers. Indeed, these fathers were three times as violent as those of the control group of nonassaultive men. But it was more than violence that helped create the difference. In analysis after analysis, the scales measuring *rejection* were more important in influencing future abusiveness than were those measuring physical abuse alone. Clearly, the emotional aspects of a father's treatment are paramount.

Shame is an emotional response to an attack on the global sense of self. When we are shamed, our very sense of who we are is threatened. And so, I also developed a twenty-two item "shame scale," derived from the EMBU, which I related to each man's profile as an abusive personality. In my research, evidence of shaming came out loud and clear: Wife assaulters had experienced childhoods characterized by global attacks on their selfhood, humiliation, embarrassment, and shame. Their parents would often publicly humiliate them or punish them at random. Often such parents would say, "You're no good. You'll never amount to anything." The integrity of the child's self came under attack.

Indeed, I found that shaming experiences, primarily by the father, were strongly related to adult rage, post-traumatic stress disorder symptoms, and to intimate partners' reports of abusiveness. The results were so significant that, if I had to pick a single parental action that generated abusiveness in men, I would say it's being shamed by their fathers. Of course, fathers who shame their sons also tend to be physically abusive, so the boy not only sustains an attack on the self but also experiences abuse-modeling.

It is, however, statistically possible to separate being physically abused from being shamed. This enables us to look at the direct effects of shame on adult abusiveness as though physical abuse had not occurred. When I did this, I found that shaming experiences were still strongly related to the development of the abusive personality and to rage. The opposite, however, was not true. Paternal physical abuse by itself did not predict anger or even abusiveness. The lethal combination of shaming and physical abuse was required. Unfortunately, that combination was the rule rather than the exception.

As a result of my studies, I have found that the biggest childhood contributors to wife assault, in order of importance, are: feeling rejected by one's father, feeling a lack of warmth from one's father, being physically abused by one's father, being verbally abused by one's father, and feeling rejected by one's mother. (I had expected that the relationship with mother would have been the more important, but that wasn't the case.) A cold, absent, and intermittently abusive and shaming father produces a boy with a weak sense of identity (also known as *identity diffusion*).

This is a climate that seems to destroy the soul, a climate wherein the central message is the unworthiness of the self. What if this climate had persisted since birth for these boys? This is not farfetched, for research indicates that much violence begins in early childhood.[3] If the identities of these boys is not nurtured, a stable, positive sense of who they are cannot develop.

■ The Power of Shame

A father's shaming is the worst thing that can happen to a boy—far worse than simply being reprimanded for misbehavior. Shame is a generalized corrosive punishment of the self rather than a punishment of the act. Being told "You're no good" or "You'll never amount to anything," teaches the child that he is worthless in a way that "I don't like what you did, but I love you all the same" never does. Indeed, anything a father does to imbue a sense of shame has important and lifelong ramifications for his son. Shame is experienced as an attack on the whole self, and shaming incidents are long remembered.

Assailing a youngster in front of others has the terrible effect of public humiliation. The child is overcome with an intolerable discomfort; his very being is open to ridicule by others. As Lenore Terr puts it in her excellent book on childhood trauma, *Too Scared to Cry*, shame comes from "public exposure of one's own vulnerability."[4] Others have defined humiliation as a loss of control over one's identity.[5]

Punishing a child at random is equally pernicious. The boy cannot determine what specifically he has done wrong to deserve the punishment. The effect is to generalize the "wrongness" to the whole self. The shaming aspect of punishment runs deep and conveys a lingering message: that the boy is repulsive, contemptible, and unlovable in a global sense. By obscuring the connection between behavior and castigation, the randomly shaming and punishing father attacks the boy's identity.

Mike, my withdrawn, depressed client who complained of nightmares, finally revealed to the group one of the ways that he had been abused. He would be relaxing, just watching television, when his father would sneak up from behind and suddenly punch him in the head. He never knew when it was coming. He never knew what he had done, what specific act triggered the punishment. Thus, he started to feel that he was being penalized for being himself—from his father's behavior, he learned that his whole self was "bad."

Punishment of the self creates what psychiatrist Leonard Sheingold describes as "soul murder." This term refers to the "shutting off of all emotion, often by using autohypnosis," which occurs in abused children largely to defend themselves against their hurt and rage at the perpetrator.[6] They must acquiesce, since any indication of their rage in their father's presence could prove lethal.

Although Sheingold is talking about cases of severe ongoing

sexual or physical abuse, it may be that shaming attacks on the self generate similar responses. By comparison, punishments that are neither public, random, nor humiliating do not seem to carry such a permanent imprimatur.

In his classic *The Art of Loving*, Eric Fromm describes mother love as "the home we come from, nature, soil, the ocean."[7] All yearning for connection is the longing to return to the perfect, all-embracing love. Father's love, on the other hand, is conditional. Fromm characterizes it as earned or deserved love carrying an unspoken message, "I love you because you fulfill my expectations, because you do your duty, because you are like me." Fatherly love sets limits, punishes, rewards, and judges.

Unfortunately, abusive or rejecting fathers create expectations that are unfulfillable, or they simply up the ante if the child succeeds in meeting their demands. These fathers have a need to punish. In the act of assailing their child, they solidify their own shaky sense of self. And so, the child is doomed. He cannot please, nothing is ever good enough for Papa. The boy feels unlovable to the main source of his male identity.

■ The Conspiracy of Silence

Oscar had shamed and humiliated Ignacio. He had denigrated him, beaten him, rendered him powerless, and threatened him with death. Yet, when I first inquired about his stepfather, Ignacio had said, "He was an all right guy, pretty good to me sometimes." Oscar's behavior isn't unusual in this regard. In fact, most clinicians who ask wife assaulters about their parents report similar responses.

Some people believe that abusive men will eagerly recount their maltreatment at the hands of their fathers or make up stories as a way of gaining sympathy or exonerating themselves for their current behavior. If that were the case, we would see inflated depictions of terrible early family lives. Yet, in actuality, these men rarely speak of it. Like battered women, they tend to idealize their families and paint rosy pictures of their childhoods that only darken with probing. Their lack of emotional articulateness is startling. What can account for this reticence?

In *When a Child Kills*, lawyer Paul Mones explains that the most difficult cases for him to defend were those in which boys had killed their father or stepfather: The boys didn't want to talk about the abuse they had suffered and would steadfastly defend the parent.[8] This strange loyalty has been likened to the paradoxical bonds that form between hostages and victims in the Stockholm syndrome (see Chapter 3).[9] It is a survival strategy.

Interestingly, our research found that assaultive men whom the courts send to our research and treatment team would also idealize their parents' treatment of them. It wasn't until we mathematically cleansed their self-report questionnaires for *socially desirable responding* (a tendency to deny faults or portray oneself in a positive light) that a closer approximation of the truth came out.

This process of hiding is also true in group therapy. Early in treatment, men euphemize. Like Ignacio, they describe their fathers as "stern" or "strict." They say, "Dad had a bad temper sometimes," or "He wasn't around much; I guess he liked fishing more," or "The folks did the best they could under the circumstances." Only when I dig deeper and ask specifically, "What did your dad do when he was angry?" or "How did your father show you that he loved you? Can you remember any specific time that he did this?" did a more horrifying story emerge.

My conversation with Robert, the deep-sea diver, went something like this:

"My dad had a bad temper sometimes."

"What did he do?"

"Well, he used to yell a lot."

"Who did he yell at?"

"Me and my mom."

"What did he say when he was yelling?"

"Well, you know, put-down kinds of things."

"Can you remember anything specific?"

Robert paused. "Well, he used to tell me that I would never amount to anything, that I was a loser and I'd always be a loser."

"Did you ever see him hit your mom?"

"No, but I heard things."

"What kind of things?"

"Well, yelling and screaming, and sometimes I knew there was a fight."

"A fight?"

"Yeah, I mean a physical thing."

"You heard him hit her?"

"Well, yeah."

As a child, the abused boy unconsciously feels ashamed of what goes on in the home but he learns to cover up. He masks his feelings from everyone, including himself. He never invites friends over and secretly envies their home lives. He tries hard to put the shame underground, to bury it. But it never stays hidden. The hellhounds of emotional crisis root it out. Each peccadillo threatens to reopen the chasm of shame. It is for this reason that the boy so relentlessly casts blame outside himself. To accept blame risks too much.

Moreover, he is aided and abetted by a socializing culture that for centuries has taught men not to be emotionally expressive—that's only for wimps. The double burden of shame and cultural conditioning makes him retreat to his inner world. Safely ensconced there, he unconsciously begins the task of expunging every possible source of shame from his identity. Men have cosmetically altered everything from a "lower class" accent to racial identity in fleeing shame.

According to his sister, the entertainer Michael Jackson grew up in an abusive home.[10] Each operation he has for his "skin condition" makes him look more white. And Teresa Carpenter's *Esquire* investigation of O. J. Simpson's life tells of his father leaving the family when O. J. was barely more than a toddler. Abandonment is the ultimate rejection, and O. J.'s deepest sources of shame may have included poverty, physical infirmity, and his father's open homosexuality.[11]

As a child, O. J. suffered from rickets and wore braces. Neighborhood kids called him "Pencil Pins." He admitted in an earlier *Playboy* magazine interview that he was "very sensitive" about these taunts. The early wound was there. Then he discovered his escape from early shame; he could run fast with a football. He slowly reinvented himself, erasing his "black" speech patterns and eventually leaving his black wife for a blonde white woman. It would seem that he didn't feel black pride.

Still, the early wounds to the ego wouldn't disappear. O. J. needed constant reaffirmation and adulation in order to know who he was. He felt "alone and lost" on a 1975 vacation in Paris because, in his words, "I was just another tourist who didn't speak the language. Nobody knew me."[12]

It is not unusual for an abusive man to be unable to recall his childhood. His upbringing is hazy, often with long erasures from his memory tapes. The therapist must piece his past together by asking him probing questions, by interviewing his wife (who usually knows the most), and occasionally by meeting with his mother (who may or may not be forthcoming).

When I started to collect questionnaire data on abusive men I found the same problem with fuzzy memories. Men who initially balk at filling out a scale measuring violence in their family of origin would subsequently turn out to be the ones who suffered the most abuse. They had blanked out or blurred the memories. They would complain to the researcher that they couldn't remember. They would resist filling out the questionnaires. They would repeatedly "forget" to bring them in. They would get angry at the questions asked.

These men were generally more positive about their mothers, although their responses revealed a sense of alternating warm and cold currents. Mother was available at some times; at others, she was cold or angry. (I suspect, although I cannot prove it from my data, that these women were frequently trying to provide maternal support while coping with an abusive husband. It's not surprising to me that they were not always able to succeed.)

I found that not only had these men been shamed as children, but now, as adults, they are ashamed of that humiliation, heaping shame upon shame. People who have been exposed to shame will do anything to avoid it in the future. They blame others for their behavior. The pain of revisiting the trauma is so great that they have never been remotely willing to examine it. The result is a man who sometimes needs affection but cannot ask for it, is sometimes vulnerable but can't admit it, and is often hurt by some small symbol of lack of love but can only criticize. It is a man who can describe none of these feelings and has forgotten or repressed their source.

■ The Shame-Prone Personality

Another clue to the nature of these childhood traumatic experiences comes through the work of social psychologist June Tangney. Drawing on earlier work on "humiliated fury" and "the shame-rage spiral," Tangney developed a test in which respondents described which of several reactions they would experience to a variety of everyday mishaps. Tangney differentiated between people whom she called "guilt-prone" and those who were "shame-prone." The former accept blame for a mishap but see it as an isolated mistake.

The shame-prone individual, on the other hand, regards every mishap as indicative of a general flaw in themselves. They cannot make the distinction between a specific mistake and their overarching imperfection. Not surprisingly, this emotional style is accompanied by "hostility, anger arousal, and tendencies to blame others for negative events."[13]

Shaming creates a vulnerable sense of self, one that can be easily attacked. The shame-prone person feels the first flashes of humiliation at the slightest affront and responds quickly with open rage or humiliated fury. This rage appears so out of proportion precisely because it is being used to prevent *idiocide*, a feeling of death of the self that has already been weakened through earlier attacks. As one of psychiatrist Leon Wurmser's patients put it, "I have never been myself except in anger."[14]

The title of Wurmser's book, *The Mask of Shame*, conveys that the exposed, vulnerable self forces one to hide behind a mask. The word *shame* comes from the Old High German root *scama* meaning "to cover oneself." Anger, of course, provides such a mask and externalizing blame protects the individual from having to reexperience the shame. Both are hallmarks of the abusive personality.

■ Humiliation and Rage

In his book *The Seductions of Crime*, UCLA criminologist Jack Katz sees the common underpinning of humiliation and rage.[15] He believes that this accounts for the rapid transformation from the first state to the second. In both, the individual experiences himself as an object compelled by forces beyond his control. When a person is humiliated, he loses hold of his identity. He becomes an object of ridicule. As Katz puts it, "Suddenly, he realizes that his identity has been transformed by forces outside his control in some fundamental way. He has become morally impotent, unable to govern the evolution of his identity."[16]

Similarly with anger, the perpetrator says, "I got carried away, I didn't know what I was doing." He expresses the rage as somehow external to and taking over his life. Both are holistic feelings experienced as transcending bodily limitations. In humiliation, the person is overcome with an intolerable discomfort, his very being is mortified. Rage, too, "draws the whole body to its service."

According to Katz, the conversion of humiliation to rage is swift because one is the mirror opposite of the other: Humiliation is the experience of being reduced to a lower position. "In humiliation, one feels incompetent and powerless as if one's stature has been reduced to that of a baby. . . . Humiliation becomes rage when a person senses that the way to resolve the problem . . . is to turn the structure of his humiliation on its head."[17] That is, one puts oneself in a superior position when enraged.

Humiliation works from the top of the head down. We blush and then feel a sinking sensation in the abdomen. In contrast, rage proceeds in an upward direction, starting in the belly and working its way up until we "blow our top" or "rise up" in anger.

■ Shame and the Abusive Personality

Early upbringing plays a major part in formation of the self. At young, vulnerable ages, children are open and susceptible to the vicissitude of family function and dysfunction. The impact of experiences such as violence between parents, angry divorce, rejection, and shaming can take a toll on every part of the child, from his self-concept, to his ability to self-soothe or tolerate aloneness, to his capacity to modulate anger and anxiety, to the elaboration of opiate receptors in the brain,[18] and finally to his compulsive need to externalize blame because accepting responsibility reactivates the mortification.

At every level, from the physiological-neurological to the psychological, the abused/rejected boy is primed to use violence. This is not merely the learning or copying of an action that occurs in violent families, it is the configuration of an entire personality.

That configuration lays the foundation for the abusive personality. It creates certain pathways, ways of responding that will lead to further reinforcement for abuse: rage with girlfriends, possessiveness, selection of male friends who tolerate or even praise the violent streak.

As the "preabusive" boy enters his teen years, he passes from a latency period, when girls are irrelevant, to a new phase of life with peer groups and messages from the culture and his subculture about what it means to be a man. I believe that abused/rejected boys interpret and accept this information differently, even seek out different information. The message they want to hear is the one that tells them they're all right, that their anger is justified, that women are the problem. As the adolescent moves from failed relationship to failed relationship, he creates a self-fulfilling prophesy filled with fear and loathing that leads him to expect women to be disloyal, untrustworthy, and in need of control.

There is a pool of rage and shame in such an individual that can find no expression—that is, until an intimate relationship occurs, and with it the emotional vulnerability that menaces his equilibrium, the mask he has so carefully crafted over the years. Perhaps it is the mask of a "tough guy," or a "cool guy," or a "gentleman." Whatever identity he had created is irrelevant. Now a woman threatens to go backstage and see him and his shame without the makeup. Then, to his own surprise, the rage starts. He feels it like an irritation, and sometimes like a tidal wave.

He is shocked and surprised. He may apologize and feel shame immediately after, but he can't sustain that emotion; it's too painful, too reminiscent of hurts long buried. So he blames it on her. If it happens repeatedly with more than one woman, he goes from blaming her to blaming "them." His personal shortcomings become rationalized by an evolving misogyny. This misogyny then feeds on itself, contributing further to his rage with women.

At this point the abusiveness is hardwired into the system. The man is programmed for intimate violence. No woman on earth can save him, although some will try.

6 Ambivalent and Angry Attachment: The Mother's Contribution

SAM LOOKED ASHEN. HE HAD COME TO SEE ME PRIVATELY ABOUT a matter he did not want to discuss over the phone. Sam was a pleasant looking, graying man in his late forties who ran a construction company. The event that terrified him so had occurred three weeks earlier, after he had put away a few beers with his wife and some acquaintances at a neighborhood tavern on a Sunday afternoon. That was the last thing he remembered.

"The next thing I knew," he told me, "I was waking up at 4:00 A.M. Monday morning. My wife was gone and my house was destroyed. I know I must have done it, but I don't know what happened."

Bonnie did. She called Sam the following day and met him at a restaurant, where she told him she was afraid of him and was leaving. She recounted the incident: He had "gone off" about dinner being cooked a certain way. He had screamed at her and pushed her. He had ripped the banisters off their moorings with his bare hands, punched her repeatedly, and thrown a meat cleaver and the pan of steaks she was frying at her as she ran out the door. She told him it was the scariest thing she had ever experienced.

Sam maintained that nothing like that had ever happened before. He remembered the men at the bar were complaining about their marriages and women in general. He and Bonnie had smiled knowingly at each other, feeling they had transcended these problems.

But as our conversation progressed and Sam described his childhood, a clearer picture began to take shape. He portrayed his mother as cold, controlling, and manipulative. He expressed a deep hatred for her. "I left home at thirteen," he explained, "after my mom moved in with another man while my dad was bedridden in the hospital. Do you think that might have something to do with what happened to me and Bonnie that night?"

Indeed, I did. A man's early relationship with his mother is the second key element in the evolution of the abusive personality.

■ Of Monkeys and Mothers

During the 1960s and 1970s, experimental psychologist Harry Harlow and his wife, M. K. Harlow, spent years investigating the social development and bonding behaviors of rhesus monkeys.[1] In a now classic group of studies, they constructed inanimate replicas or surrogates of mother monkeys made of cuddly soft cloth or inhospitable wire mesh. In one experiment, they created "evil" surrogates that emitted noxious blasts of air, extruded brass spikes, hurled the baby monkeys to the floor, or vibrated so violently as to make the infants' teeth chatter.

Surprisingly, none of these hardships disrupted the baby monkeys' bonding behavior. Despite the odiousness of the "evil" surrogate mothers, the infants clung to them ever more tenaciously. This led the Harlows to conclude that, ironically, "instead of producing experimental neurosis, we have achieved a technique for enhancing maternal attachment."[2] In effect, the Harlows had created an artificial model of child abuse in which comfort is intermittently disrupted by toxic behavior. To their astonishment, rather than weakening the attachment process, the abuse had strengthened it.

Psychological theories about the sources of intimate rage trace its origins to very early mother-infant traumas that are, perhaps, more subtle than those the Harlows' monkeys had withstood, but no less devastating. These experiences are replete with feelings of yearning, frustration, and abandonment, with love, fear, and rage, and they inscribe themselves indelibly in the psyches of wife abusers.

■ Normal Separation and Individuation

In my quest to understand how and why a cyclical abuser's personality splits into two highly distinct behavior patterns, and why he sees his wife alternatively as a Madonna or a whore, I turned to the psychiatric theories that explain normal personality development. Whereas Freud emphasized the oedipal stage, which begins around age three, later psychiatry has focused on the pre-oedipal period as more important for the formation of personality.

Object relations is a theory explaining how infants form first relationships with those who care for them. First developed by psychiatrists Melanie Klein and Joan Riviere in the 1930s,[3] it has been elaborated by others, including psychoanalyst Margaret Mahler at the Masters Childrens Center in New York, and it addresses the issue of the split.

According to object relations theory, as we wander for the first time from our mother's embrace, our basic notions of selfhood develop. It gradually dawns on us that we are a separate entity from our mother. Mahler has described this awareness as the "psychological birth of the human infant."[4] It is also not a coincidence that rage is born and temper tantrums appear during this period.

When an infant becomes a toddler and can walk away from his mother (at age ten to fourteen months), some dramatic changes occur in his emotional world. He begins to exhibit a growing awareness of separation; he realizes that he is on his own. As this awareness flourishes during the next period (between fifteen and twenty-four months), the infant seems to have an increased need for his mother to share with him every one of his new skills and experiences. His need for closeness, held in abeyance throughout the previous developmental period, becomes evident at the very time he is developing the capability to create physical distance between himself and his mother.

Mahler calls this the *rapprochement subphase of individuation*. As she puts it, "One cannot emphasize too strongly the importance of optimal emotional availability of the mother during this subphase."[5] At this stage, the infant alternately searches for and avoids body contact with his mother. He shadows her, incessantly watching and following her every move, and then scampers away.

With this behavior, the child indicates his deep ambivalence: He wants to reunite with the one he loves but at the same time fears she will reengulf him. On the other hand, he enjoys his new freedom but doesn't want to lose his mother. The toddler begins to learn that he is not omnipotent, but instead small and dependent. Yet, since his newfound autonomy is so exciting, he denies or suppresses his dependency. And so, as Mahler explains, this period is "characterized by the rapidly alternating desire to push mother away and to cling to her."[6]

In his actions, the child expresses this inner conflict as intense demandingness and clinginess alternating with equally intense negativity and battling. In truth, it is his first experience with the paradoxical demands of intimacy—to be oneself and yet be part of a relationship—with all the ambivalence that this engenders.

A toddler's ability to tolerate separation from his mother depends on his developing inner representations of her. If his inner image is of a warm, nurturant mother, that is sufficient to sustain ordinary periods of separation. When he wanders afield, he holds this internal image of her and knows he can safely return to her whenever he wants. This stable inner representation of mother is called *object constancy*. When properly attained, the child develops a secure, consistent, positive sense of a mother soothing him. Later on he is able to soothe himself by activating this inner representation. Because of this ability, he can keep tension from building.

If, however, the mother is unavailable, the toddler invests too much energy in "wooing her" and doesn't have enough left for the next developmental steps. Conversely, if she is too anxious and begins shadowing *him*, she intrudes upon him and he cannot separate. He literally forces his attention to the outside world to avoid this intrusion and cannot easily return to mother. In either case, the inner notion of a stable lovable self is impaired.

Of course, mothers may not take kindly to their toddlers separating. As Mahler explains, "The mothers' reaction at that time was often tinged with feelings of annoyance at the toddlers' insistence on his autonomy."[7]

This is a normal impulse. But I wonder how a mother, abused by her husband, can possibly proffer all of the crucial and sensitively tuned responses that her baby requires. She may, for example, find "optimal emotional availability" difficult to provide constantly. This developmental aspect of abusiveness has been generally overlooked, despite its important ramifications for the development of a rageful self.

Around twenty-one months "the clamoring for omnipotent control, the extreme periods of separation anxiety, the alternation of demands for closeness and autonomy" subside and each child begins to find an *optimal distance* from his mother. Mahler defines this as "the distance at which he could function best."[8] It is a compromise between separation anxiety (if too far from mother) and engulfment (if too close).

Mahler extended this concept to the human lifespan by viewing life as a dance between the desire for autonomy and the desire for fusion. Put somewhat differently, relationship issues become those of optimal distance. Too little distance carries a threat of reengulfment and identity loss; too much carries abandonment and loss of the other.

Compare these notions of optimal distance with my research on wife assaulters. The men I studied reacted with unbridled anxiety and anger to videotaped scenarios of "abandonment" that seemed innocuous to other men. Departures from their comfort zones for optimal distance produced the most extreme rage in assaultive men—literally off the scale. They also have personality deficits that render them most susceptible to dependency on and anxiety about relationship loss. Given assaultive males' typical emotional isolation and their exaggerated dependence on their intimate partners, their panic and hysterical aggression are the psychological result of perceived loss of the female.

I believe that the roots of such emotional patterns may be found during this separation-individuation phase. My hunch is that a consequence of an assaultive husband is a mother who cannot possibly balance the difficult demands of this process. In this way, the father's physical abusiveness, even when it is not directed at the son, has important ramifications for the boy's personality, not just his behavior.

Moreover, since an incomplete rapprochement task plagues abusive men, there are certain similarities in their childhood and adult behaviors. These include the inability to use language in a way that produces a sense of control, or as we call it in adults, *spouse-specific assertiveness*. Instead, these men are either extremely unassertive, leading to occasional explosions (like the overcontrolled batterer described in Chapter 2) or they become dominators who use every form of control (financial, emotional, physical) instead of negotiation.

Because their ability to play is lost, adults with remnants of rapprochement conflict tend to lose sight of themselves in intimate relationships. They experience anxiety about closeness and separation, poor spouse-specific assertiveness, and poor tolerance of aloneness (or conversely high dependency).

Assaultive men present this very profile. They search for

women they can dominate, especially in the sense of dictating the emotional distance in the relationship, perhaps as a way of finally managing the original trauma of a failed rapprochement. When we try to control something, usually anxiety and anger lie behind our behavior. When that control is threatened, the hidden anxiety and anger quickly surface.

Consider Ignacio, whom I introduced in Chapter 5. This adolescent boy, convicted in his stepfather's killing, had suffered directly and indirectly from family violence. In interviewing his mother, Rosa, I discovered that she was one of ten children in a family of migrant farm laborers. She began working at age three. She described her family as very strict; her father beat her if she skipped school. She ran away from home at seventeen to live with the father of her oldest child, Inez. When he abandoned her, she returned to her family, but they threw her out. She worked in the fields, leaving her baby daughter in the car.

This arrangement continued until Rosa was nineteen, when she met and married Ignacio's father, Francisco. Rosa described life with him as "pure hell." He was highly abusive, beating at first her and Inez, and then Ignacio as well. Unbeknownst to her, he had also sexually molested Inez between the ages of three and five. Rosa left him because of the violence and his drug use. (In a separate interview, Ignacio recalled Rosa shooting Francisco in both ankles with a pistol.)

That's when she met Oscar. He had been given up for adoption at the age of three weeks and had been abused by his adoptive mother. Rosa described Oscar as a loner and a perfectionist. Of course, Oscar, as we know, hit and threatened Ignacio, but he also turned his wrath against Rosa and Inez, beating both of them and pushing Rosa down when she was six months pregnant. Yet Rosa covered for Oscar's violence and wouldn't leave him because "he paid the bills."

How is it feasible, in a family as dysfunctional as this, for a mother to be attuned to her child's subtle needs? Indeed, how can she be available at all? Under what circumstances could Ignacio develop a stable sense of his mother's warmth and loving care? It seems an impossible task. I have heard that Ignacio, after having served his time for killing his stepfather, has had flashes of rage at his girlfriend and has even beaten her. Can anyone be surprised at this turn?

■ Love and Rage: Madonnas and Whores

In their book *Love, Hate and Reparation*, Melanie Klein and Joan Riviere explain that the initial relationship between the infant and his mother provides the origins of rage.[9] As Klein puts it, "For the infant child, the mother is the original and most complete source of satisfaction of the totality of wants and pleasures. Yet this total pleasure is inevitably frustrated."[10]

A baby who is nursing and nurtured is unaware of his dependency. In fact, according to Klein and Riviere, he recognizes only his own existence and fully expects all of his needs to be fulfilled. If they're not, he discovers that he is truly dependent—he can't survive on his own. "He cries and screams. . . . He automatically explodes, as it were, with hate and aggressive craving. If he feels emptiness and loneliness, an automatic reaction sets in, which may soon become uncontrollable and overwhelming. . . . The baby's world is out of control . . . and this is because he loves and desires."[11] According to Klein and Riviere, adult hate and aggression (and perhaps even the tantrums that abused women describe) all derive from this developmental period when identity issues first form.

Since his existence depends entirely on his mother, the child experiences this frustration as a threatened destruction of his entire self. Frustration coupled with such severe consequences generates strong reactions, notably rage, hatred, and a wish to annihilate the "bad object"—his mother. But the child must defend against these destructive fantasies and impulses since their expression could jeopardize his relationship with the very person who sustains his life. He must control the original rage, because to display it or even feel it risks devastation. Mother, if she detects it, could sever the lifeline.

In order to control the rage, the child develops survival mechanisms called *primitive defenses* (so called because they occur early in life). One, basic to psychological growth, is that of *splitting* or dividing the object or mother into good and bad parts. The "good mother" or *good object* is all-loving and gratifying whereas the "bad mother" or *bad object* is withholding and absent. By preserving this distinction, the child can entertain fantasies of rage toward the "bad mother" without risk of destroying the "good mother."

In normal development, these two aspects eventually fuse. Mother is both bad and good. Sometimes, however, this process gets derailed, and when it does, an integrated view of the mother cannot develop. What remains from this splitting are two segregated perceptions: one mother who is ideal and nourishing and another who is punitive, withholding, and thus destructive. In other words, the object is not constant, but alternately all good or all bad.

Without a constant, nourishing object, the child develops an insecure, inconsistent, and negative sense of self. He cannot soothe himself or handle stress well. And at times, this inability to self-soothe allows tension to build, with the sense of a volcanic eruption from within, of a self about to fly apart.

These reactions persist into adulthood, but lie dormant until another relationship carries similar emotional threats and promises. Intimate romantic relationships are the closest a man comes to re-creating his early union with his mother. The extreme, out of control nature of an infant's rage mirrors battered women's descriptions of their husband's tantrums. In fact, this excessive violence in adults is often referred to as *infantile rage*.

The division of mother into unintegrated parts may also constitute the later yoking of the Dr. Jekyll (good, unaggressive, socialized) self to the Mr. Hyde (bad, aggressive, abusive, uncontrolled) self. The two parts are not integrated, and, to the extent that they appear in different situations, they leave one (and one's partner) with the confusing task of reconciling two different selves. No wonder the women complain, "He's like two different people." In truth, he is.

The vague but deep terror of disintegration is a constant experience in persons with an unstable sense of object constancy. For the abusive man, aloneness is terrifying and any prospect of abandonment is horrific. He needs the other person to provide an emotional glue that keeps his self intact, keeps him together, soothes him. His rage fuses his self; the anger overrides the feeling of coming apart. However, its aftermath and the woman's threat to leave re-creates this feeling. At the same time, being socialized into a male culture where such feelings are unacceptable, his terror is submerged and stifled until it becomes a distant presence—the proverbial beast hidden in the basement of the subconscious, tearing at the lock on the flimsy door to the main floor where everyday life is lived.

This is the psychological basis for the sleep disturbances, the nightmares, the feelings of vague dysphoria. This man senses something isn't right; he feels the diffuse tension, but he can't name it. Anguish is a recurring demon, depression and anxiety frequent experiences. Usually these are blotted out by alcohol or drugs, which override the more painful feelings.

When the beast of terror finally succeeds in breaking down the door, the man rages at his wife or punches her. He rids himself of the feelings temporarily. Fury is the magic elixir that restores an inner sense of power. In an instant, the powerlessness and jealousy evaporate; the accumulating tension dissipates. But if he drives his partner away, the terror worsens and manifests itself in extreme actions to get her back, including threats of suicide.[12] Recall Robert's overwrought state when his wife left him over the incident with the key.

The concept of splitting provides a way to explain why the abusive man either idealizes or devalues his intimate partners. One week she's impossible and life with her is living hell. The next week she's a "good woman" and it was he who was wrong. When in his normal phase, the assaultive man is unable to assert intimacy needs or dissatisfactions. As tension and feelings of being unloved and unappreciated build, his "rageful self" (split off or hidden outside of consciousness) begins to emerge and his view of his wife becomes increasingly negative.

In this phase, he ruminates on the concept of his wife as a wanton woman. She is unfaithful, sexually promiscuous, malevolent, and unloving—a whore. The whore is the recipient of all the repressed rage and sexuality originally reserved for the "bad mother." Fear of the bad mother and of his own rage haunts the person whose object relations are disturbed. Men in treatment groups call this rumination playing the bitch tape. It doesn't stop until the rage explodes.

After the abuse and the release of tension, this self-absorbed ego-inflation always collapses into a sense of unworthiness. The man idealizes his mate and devalues himself. Once in the contrition phase, he becomes temporarily docile, almost servile. Now he puts his wife on a pedestal. Suddenly she has become the "good mother"—the Madonna. (I am reminded of Gloria Steinem's dictum: "A pedestal is as much a prison as any other small space.") At this stage, he remains temporarily at her knees.

Projection, a second type of primitive defense, goes further in explaining the abuser's behavior. Projection is a safety valve that helps us avoid pain, threat, or helplessness. Rather than take responsibility for these unpleasant feelings, we relocate them in others. The victim in slasher films, for example, is almost always portrayed as a sexually promiscuous female. This may be a form of projection in which the hated and repressed longing for the mother is projected onto the bad girl, who is then punished.

Projection means perceiving in the other person those aspects that we can't face in ourselves. We deny them and visualize them in someone else, usually someone close. The other becomes a blank screen for a movie that we alone write and direct.

Abusive men deny aggressive and sexual impulses in themselves, project them onto their partners, and view their partners as wicked. They perceive aggression in their wives while denying their own. They see her as flirtatious while disowning their own philandering. Their own dalliances are "what men do" but they watch their mates like a hawk for any signs of similar behavior.

According to Faye Resnick,

> The fury that possessed [O. J.] whenever [Nicole] behaved like a normal wife and partner—like complaining bitterly when he openly had sexual liaisons with other women—erupted out of his belief that she was literally his possession. O. J. was genuinely astounded at being questioned. As his rage mounted, he would turn the blame around and condemn Nicole for getting him angry, totally bypassing the issue of how he had wronged her.[13]

Resnick says that O. J. "just couldn't acknowledge anything was his fault. So everything became her fault."[14] He had refined blaming to an art.

Denial was also present, even when going through the motions of seeking psychotherapy. In response to Nicole asking if Simpson had told his therapist about the abuse, he replied, "Well, what does that have to do with anything? We're in a new era here. This is all about going forward."[15]

There is a way out of this miasma of unrealistic expectation and cyclical disappointment: to mourn the loss of what was never attained and attempt to integrate the good and bad aspects of what is still possible. However, rather than acknowledging these deep childhood losses, most abusive men turn from them and hold them in contempt. They devalue, dismiss, or run from them.

Male models for grieving are few. Terry Malloy, the character Marlon Brando played in *On the Waterfront,* laments the time he was told to fix a prizefight by taking a dive. "I coulda been a contender. I coulda been a somebody, instead of a nobody, which is what I am." Few of us, however, are willing to make this confession. Instead of feeling hurt, some men decide to get even—for life.

Men in particular seem incapable of grieving and mourning on an individual basis. Perhaps that is why the blues are so popular with men. They serve a socially sanctioned form of expression for this lost and unattainable process. Why dwell on personal loss, when it can be done vicariously through endless songs of booze, woe, and women who've caught the train and gone? When blues artist Robert Johnson sings, "I've been mistreated and I don't mind dyin'," a multitude of men can feel their own unmet yearnings and nod in assent: I'm hurt and it was her fault.

Object relations explains much about the abusive personality, but not all. For, although all boys probably experience the mother as a source of frustration and pleasure, many are able to integrate the early split and develop a secure sense of object constancy. Indeed, most men do not resort to intimate violence as adults.

Frustration and pleasure must combine in some special way for men who go through approach/destroy cycles with women in order to produce their insatiable longing and the aggressive deprecating rage. The basis of this cyclical behavior seems to be a special kind of ambivalence or alternating behavior in the mother: She mixes rejection or frustration with affection and pleasure in such a complex way that the child cannot separate, subdivide, and distribute them elsewhere. In short, the child cannot develop a consistent attitude toward the mother, nor later toward women in general.[16]

For this type of man, women will always be alluring, loving, faithless, and treacherous. For him, therefore, women are irresistible and dangerous. Fusion with mother (and by extension all women) is at the same time an ultimate source of pleasure and identity and the source of frustration and threatened destruction—a constant push and pull. To understand this phenomenon, we must look to attachment theory for answers.

■ Attachment and Power

We live the first years of our lives in total dependency on another person who has life and death power over us. As attachment is necessary for survival, the male learns early that his mother (and by association, any intimate woman) has monumental power over him.

Power differentials such as these, in and of themselves, promote bonding. They are central to the connection that occurs between victim and captor in hostage-taking situations.[17] Even the Harlows' baby rhesus monkeys attached much more intensely than normal with their intermittently abusive surrogate mothers. One reality that may differentiate boys from girls is that the former develop a stronger bond to an *opposite gender* person at an earlier developmental stage. This bond contains a sense of powerlessness that may persist into adult intimate relationships.

True emotional safety and security are initially associated with the physical presence of a woman. This may be why even men find it easier to open up with a woman. Conversely, when a mother frustrates these security needs at an early stage, the resulting emotional reaction may be extreme and long lived.

British psychiatrist John Bowlby defined attachment as a bond developed with a "preferred individual *who is conceived as stronger and/or wiser*."[18] Threats or separations to that secure attachment produce potent emotional responses such as terror, grief, and rage. These are proportional to the child's sense of the other having absolute and unrestricted power.

■ Attachment and Abandonment

In 1939, Britain had bigger problems to worry about than the nuances of mother-infant bonding. The approaching German war machine made any sense of secure bonding a forgotten ideal. Yet, in a paper to the British Psychoanalytic Society that year, Bowlby outlined his views on the type of childhood experiences that led to psychological disorders.[19] Bowlby considered the most important aspects of early childhood to be a mother's emotional attitude toward her child and a child's prolonged separations from her.

MOTHER'S ATTITUDES

In Bowlby's investigations, mother's attitudes became apparent in how she handled the feeding, weaning, toilet training, and other daily aspects of child care. Most mothers were loving in their interactions but some demonstrated an unconscious hostility toward the child. This showed up in small signs of dislike such as "unnecessary deprivations and frustrations, in impatience over naughtiness, in odd words of bad temper, in a lack of sympathy and understanding which the usually loving mother intuitively has."

These were accompanied by an overprotective attitude designed to compensate for the hostility: "being afraid to let the child out of their sight, fussing over minor illness, worrying lest something terrible should happen to their darlings."[20]

Later, in a landmark series of books entitled *Attachment and Loss*, Bowlby argued that human attachment was of paramount importance for emotional growth.[21] It serves a vital biological function indispensable for the infant's survival. In his view, the need for secure attachment rivals feeding and mating in importance. It is essential.

Reactions to the satisfaction or dissatisfaction of early attempts at attachment set up in children lifelong attachment styles. These are whole constellations of thoughts and feelings about intimacy, and they differ as mothers' attachment behaviors differ.

Bowlby's ideas take into account children's individual differences. He described attachment styles as being either secure, dismissing, or fearful. Secure youngsters are comfortable with closeness. Those who are dismissing tend to be wary of and stay out of relationships. Children who are fearfully attached divide into two subgroups. One group is clingy and preoccupied with the romantic partner's reaction. The other exhibits an ambivalence toward intimacy and to those with whom they are emotionally connected. The push-pull reaction of fearful attachment resembles the ebb and flow of the cyclical personality.

Attachment is governed by three important principles: alarm, contact, and, if contact is frustrated, anger. Whenever the child is stressed or alarmed, he walks or crawls toward his mother and seeks soothing physical contact. Only this will terminate the alarm; nothing else will do. If the attachment system is activated for a long time without that contact, angry behavior erupts. *The original motive for anger is to reestablish soothing contact.* Anger is a last-ditch effort, after other approaches have failed. A fundamental conclusion of attachment theory is that *anger follows unmet attachment needs.*

In abusive adults, self-generated tension cycles eerily resemble attachment processes in children. The tension builds from within but the man does not express his need for soothing. When contact is not forthcoming, rage results.

According to Bowlby, if a mother rebuffs or threatens her child, that intensely activates his attachment systems. Only physical contact with her will calm him. If shortly thereafter, she permits him access, no lasting conflict situation is created. On the other hand, if physical contact with her infant is distasteful to the mother (because of some acute trauma, unresolved anger, or the infant's personality), she will block his access. The resultant conflict within the infant is then serious, deep, and nonverbal.

The recognition of his mother's inaccessibility further activates the system, and if the child is not soothed, he becomes angry. If this occurs repeatedly, attachment-anger develops. This is a lifelong style of reacting to intimacy with anger.

SEPARATIONS

Anger is a common childhood response to extended separations from one's mother. Observers have noted significant differences in hostile play between separated and nonseparated children.[22] Separated children attack parent dolls. They express their anger intermittently and often intersperse it with affection, the hallmark of ambivalence. Bowlby found that separated children or those who have suffered some disruption of the attachment bond respond with ambivalence toward their mothers for up to twenty weeks after reunion.

Bowlby also noted that when a child is first separated from his mother, he becomes acutely angry and distressed. He tries to bring her back by crying loudly, shaking his crib, throwing himself about, and looking eagerly toward anything that might be her. His behavior suggests his expectation that she will return.[23]

Loud crying and the shaking of the crib are early forms of later physical acts we would call aggressiveness. As Bowlby put it, "When a relationship to a special loved person is endangered, we are not only anxious but are usually angry as well. . . . As responses to the risk of loss, anxiety and anger go hand in hand. . . . When a child or spouse behaves dangerously, an angry protest is likely to deter. When a lover's partner strays, a sharp reminder how much he or she cares may work wonders."[24]

Anger is the first phase of a child's reaction to separation. It is an "anger born of fear"—the fear of loss. The anger is designed to magically re-create that lost object or prevent her disappearance. It is a way to signal and control. Bowlby explains that in the right time and place and to the proper degree, anger can be indispensable in deterring dangerous behavior, driving away a rival, or coercing a partner. In each case, the purpose of the anger is to protect a cherished relationship.

Maladaptive violence is the distorted and exaggerated manifestation of this potentially functional emotion. By adulthood, the abusive male has learned to reshape these actions over a lifetime.

He has replaced crying by shouting, by shaking the crib, by throwing or smashing objects, by thrashing about, by punching. At these junctures, his suppressed dependency explodes in a pyrotechnic display of rage and desperation. But even if his behaviors have changed, the motive is the same—they are an attempt to regain control of the separation through physical actions.

Only after the infant's prolonged failure to bring his mother back will the subsequent emotions of depression and eventual detachment appear. Once a cyclically abusive man realizes that the anger and violence have failed, and his wife or lover is leaving, this produces a deep depression and even suicidal or homicidal threats or actions. The depression replicates the mourning seen in young children after their anger has failed to make their mothers return. The violence seems to be the only escape for these bad feelings.

Bowlby foreshadows the notion that separation anxiety underlies anger in adult romantic relationships. He observes that fifteen- to eighteen-year-olds with behavioral problems seem to have been disciplined by parents who threatened to abandon them if they didn't behave. Such children become furious at their parents' threat of desertion, but they dare not express that anger for fear the parent will make good on the threat. According to Bowlby, "This is the main reason . . . why in these cases, anger at a parent usually becomes repressed and is then directed at other targets."[25]

Robert was a classic example of this. His explosion at his wife's imagined abandonment at the office party had early origins. He had been adopted as a baby. Whenever he disobeyed his adoptive parents, they threatened to "give him back." I can only guess at the repercussion these threats had on his young psyche. But as an adult, the results were intense agitation, dissociation, and outbursts of rage at the slightest hint—real or imagined—of separation.

Bowlby also anticipated the persistence of attachment issues into adulthood. When we are confident that an attachment figure will be available to us whenever we want it, we are far less apt to experience fear than would someone who lacks this assurance. "Confidence in the availability of attachment figures . . . is built up slowly during the years of immaturity—infancy, childhood, adolescence—*and whatever expectations are developed during those years tend to persist relatively unchanged throughout the rest of life.*"[26]

These expectations, or *internal representations*, of self and relationship partners are central components of one's personality. They contain a model of the self as worthy or unworthy of care and love. They generate unconscious expectations about the consequences of attachment and provide a context for later social relationships such as the trustworthiness and availability of others. They produce self-fulfilling prophecies—the expectations contained in the internal representation engender actions that repeatedly make them come true.

Unfortunately, anger itself creates distance from others. And this can intensify the sense of separation, which spawns even more anger and further alienation. For these reasons, anger in response to separation can produce an emotional spiral culminating in rage. Anger born of fear constitutes for the abusive man an important source of rage.

Mary Ainsworth experimented further with Bowlby's theories of attachment styles. She brought mothers and babies into an unfamiliar environment, watched as the young children played, briefly separated them from their mothers, and then observed the pair's behavior upon being reunited.

Infants displayed one of three types of behavior. The "secure" youngsters constantly turned around to be certain of their mothers' presence while they explored the strange room. They greeted their mothers with pleasure when she returned from her absence, stretching out their arms and molding to her body. They were relatively easy to console and were distinguished from other groups by how often they sought emotional sharing with their mothers and their ability to be comforted and calmed by her when distressed. About 62 to 75 percent of the North American middle-class population fits this category.

A second category described by Ainsworth, "anxious-avoidant" (corresponding to Bowlby's dismissing style), gives the impression of independence. These children explored the new environment without using their mother as a base. When separations occurred, anxious-avoidant infants seemed unaffected. Indeed, when their mothers returned, they avoided them. According to psychologist Robert Karen, the child seems to say, "Who needs you? I can do it on my own."[27] About 32 percent of Ainsworth's sample fit this category.

A third group, called "anxious-ambivalent" (these correspond to Bowlby's fearfully attached children), tended to cling to their mothers and resisted exploring the room on their own. They became extremely agitated upon separation, often crying inconsolably. This group typically sought contact with their mothers when she returned but *simultaneously arched away from her angrily and resisted all efforts to be soothed.*

These infants somehow incorporate anger into their terror at being abandoned by the mother. The mothers of these infants tended to be inconsistent and were the least confident at coping with early caregiving tasks.[28]

Robert Karen describes the resulting behavioral style as follows:

The ambivalent child (which represents about 10 per cent of children from middle-class U.S. homes) is desperately trying to influence [his mother]. He is hooked by the fact that she does come through on occasion. He picks up that she will respond— sometimes out of guilt—if he pleads and makes a big enough fuss. And so, he is constantly trying to hold onto her or to punish her for being unavailable. He is wildly addicted to her and to his efforts to make her change.[29]

The intensity and the need for impact that these anxious-ambivalent children display are reminiscent of the abusive personality.[30] Indeed, the anxious-ambivalent child could become the cyclical personality of the future. He is filled with rage, yet unable to express it. He possesses negative representations of himself and women but is cyclically drawn in a repetitive push-pull pattern with them. The only thing remaining to classify him as abusive is the behavior he learns to express his rage: abuse, flight, and promiscuity are three possibilities.

Men with early attachment problems are more likely to experience anxiety about regulating intimacy. Their arousal and anger originate in deep-seated apprehension about the original attachment object. Abusive males have magnified needs for control in intimate relationships. These men try to diminish their anxiety about being abandoned by exaggerated control of their female partner.

Ambivalently attached individuals seem to have a diminished capacity to form bases of social support and seek it when needed. A lifelong pattern of isolation may grow from early lessons that support from others is unreliable. Assaultive males are characteristically isolated individuals.

Moreover, gender specific expectations add to the aloneness. A boy with an absent or punitive father and a demanding but unavailable mother learns that men don't give emotional comfort, and that women appear to be supportive but are ultimately demanding and can't be trusted. As a result, he withdraws inside himself, while at the same time feeling a gnawing anger.

■ Abusiveness and Fearful Attachment

Abusive childhood experiences produce more than learned behavior patterns. They create avoidant-ambivalent or fearful bonding styles that generate tendencies to be overly demanding and angry in adult romantic relationships. In fact, such behavior patterns are built on the foundation of these bonding styles.

It was my belief that fearful attachment and adult abusiveness are related. Along with my colleague Kim Bartholomew, I set out to empirically verify this idea.[31] We tested groups of men for attachment styles and compared those scores with others measuring the potential for intimate violence and their wives' reports of domestic abuse. I was most interested in the men whose profiles indicated a fearful attachment. They experienced strong and unresolvable push-pulls in intimacy and were hypersensitive to rejection.

Interestingly, we found that the fearful men reported their relationships with their mothers to be high on both warmth and rejection. This is obviously a contradiction, but it points to the ambivalent relationship these men had with their mothers. They learned to want her and that she could fulfill their needs; on the other hand, they learned that she could be absent or unavailable or rejecting. They experienced a constant contest between clinginess and distancing.

The fearful men were the ones I thought would be most abusive, but I thought it was a misnomer to call them fearful. While fear might have been at the core of their reaction to anticipated rejection, anger was the prominent feature of their emotions and behavior. Whether this anger was a male cover-up for underlying fear or a vestige of what Bowlby called "the anger born of fear" didn't really matter. These men were "angrily attached," as if they were infants, *seeking proximity to mother and simultaneously arching angrily away*—a prototype of lifelong reactions to women.

As I suspected, these fearfully (angrily) attached men scored high on my measures of abusive personality. Their profiles also indicated high levels of chronic anger and jealousy and frequent post-traumatic stress symptoms: They didn't sleep well, became depressed and anxious, and experienced dissociative states when things seemed "unreal." Their fearful attachment scores were more highly associated with reports of abuse by their female partners than any other attachment style. In fact, from the men's attachment profiles, we were able to predict adult abusiveness with 88 percent accuracy.

In our earlier videotape studies, we had found that physically abusive males demonstrated greater arousal, anxiety, and anger while viewing conflicts in which a woman expresses her need for greater independence from the man. At the time I referred to this as abandonment anxiety; however, I had made no attempt to discern if some assaultive men showed this pattern of responding more than others. In retrospect, I believe that fearfully (angrily) attached men would have exhibited it the most.

Fearfully attached men had the highest levels of depression, anxiety, dissociative states (sometimes accompanied by rageful acting out), and sleep disturbances. They have been traumatized, probably by extreme attachment disruptions, and react with rage whenever they are in intimate relationships. As adults, they experience high levels of trauma symptoms. They have little insight into the causes of this constellation of problems and avoid seeking help, believing it will only make things worse.

Fearfully attached men experience extreme chronic anger as an inevitable by-product of attachment yet have great difficulty living without a woman. Intimacy inevitably produces anger in them. They cannot conceive of and do not understand the anger in attachment terms. They blame it instead, especially during their dysphoric phases, on their wives. "Why can't she make me feel better?" they wonder. In reality, the feeling stems, at least in part, from the inescapable emotional consequences of their own disturbed attachment. What remains in their developmental profile are the responses or action patterns through which they learn to express this anger.[32]

7 Learning the Ways of Violence

JUAN CARLOS WAS AN IMPRESSIVE-LOOKING MAN. HE HAD THAT proud aquiline presence that bespoke some Mayan blood. He was thick-necked, beefy, and powerful, built along the lines of a football guard. My cotherapist and I knew quite a bit about him from court documents and extensive interviews before he first came into the treatment group. He had grown up in El Salvador and had moved to Mexico City at age nine. At fifteen, he came to Vancouver. We knew he had been in a gang in Mexico and was a member of Los Diablos, the most notorious Hispanic gang in Vancouver. We also knew he had some weapons charges and that he had a history of violence.

We were not prepared for the man who came into the treatment group the first evening: a seemingly shy, soft-spoken, insightful man with a gentle presence. Juan Carlos said very little at first. It wasn't that his English was bad. It was fine—accented, but articulate. I had a sense of him watching and taking everything in. He had put most of his violence far behind him, but was still bedeviled by one remnant: assault directed toward Sandra.

Sandra was Juan Carlos's girlfriend and the mother of his child. She had given birth to two other sons before meeting Juan Carlos, each with a different father. She dressed plainly, wore little makeup, and had a natural beauty and calmness. During my private interview with her, she seemed self-assured, at peace with herself. She had exceptional communications skills and was a good listener and clear thinker. I thought she would have made an excellent therapist. She too looked Hispanic—dark-eyed and olive skinned—but claimed to be of Irish and Native American heritage.

Sandra said that violence erupted in their home about three times a year. She could tell when it was coming. It would start with Juan Carlos ignoring her, avoiding all eye contact. Then he would get pushy and demanding, then downright belligerent. She had called the police and charged him twice. Jealousy would trigger his rages. He would accuse her of having sex with another man. (Once it was a social worker. When I expressed surprise at this, she said, "Well, Juan was right. The guy did hit on me.")

The night of the most recent incident, Juan had been in "one of his moods" for about three days. Sandra had wanted to go out with a few women friends—something she hadn't done in months. "I needed a night off from the kids," she explained. "I felt the whole family closing in on me."

Juan immediately became suspicious. "What's his name?" he shouted. "Just tell me his name."

Sandra tried to reason with him. "There's no 'he,'" she said. "I'm just going out with Kathy and Elaine."

Juan could not be convinced. He stood straight up, grabbed a hunting knife from the table, yanked Sandra's hair back, and put the knife to her throat.

"Do you want to die?" he yelled in her face. "Tell me his name." Later, in reviewing the incident, Sandra said she thought of making up a name—anything to get him to stop. But instead, she struggled and stuck to her story, although she believed, at least for the moment, that she would die.

She started to retch, and Juan dragged her by the hair to the bathroom.

Then, as quickly as it had begun, the violence stopped. Juan dropped the knife and sank dejectedly into a bedroom chair. Then he put his head in his hands and cried.

That had been the worst episode. Since then, there had been other heated arguments, but no repeat of the threat with the knife. I asked Sandra if she was afraid of Juan.

"No," she replied, "I can stand up to him." Then she added with a hint of pride, "I've got some anger problems of my own." She then told me that she had been sexually molested on three separate occasions, by an uncle when she was three, a family friend when she was eight, and a cousin when she was thirteen. She was presently in counseling.

Sandra spoke warmly about Juan, especially his caring treatment of her three children. She revealed a soft side of him that he had tried to keep hidden in the all-male group.

So far, the interview was fairly typical. But when I asked about parents, Juan and Sandra's story became more intriguing. Sandra revealed that her parents had split up, and her father had beaten her mother. He had had an alcohol problem.

Juan's parents had also separated when he was a young child in El Salvador. His father had been extremely abusive. "You wouldn't believe how bad he was," Sandra said. "He would beat up Juan's mother, Imelda, throw her out of the house, and yell at the kids." Imelda fled to Mexico with her children to escape the violence.

At this point, Sandra looked me straight in the eye. "This is all confidential?" she asked.

I assured her that it was.

But she still hesitated. Eventually the dark secret that needed reassurance came pouring forth. While living in Mexico City, Juan was sexually abused by one of Imelda's boyfriends.

Currently both of Juan's estranged parents live in Vancouver. His father, Ernesto, who had somehow reformed himself and was no longer abusive, lived in the same apartment building as Juan and Sandra. So did Sandra's mother. When Juan started sliding into one of his "moods," Sandra would confide in and get support from Ernesto, the former abuser. Ernesto, who now lived peaceably with another woman, would take Juan aside for lengthy admonishments, *hombre a hombre*. I suspected that he felt some guilt for how his son had turned out. Clearly, though, there was strong family pressure from Ernesto and Sandra's mother for Juan to stop the violence. They served as a kind of in-house support system.

When the assault charges came down, Juan's mother tried to talk Sandra into dropping them. Sandra explained that it wasn't up to her—only the prosecution could do that. But Imelda was angry. She felt that Sandra wasn't standing by her man. She wouldn't speak to Sandra for months, exhibiting both family loyalty and the strange attitude that some battered women hold toward other battered women. The need to justify their own choices makes them extremely judgmental of battered women who don't behave the way they do.

This family's history, back three generations on both sides—as far back as anyone could remember—was filled with violence and abuse.

■ Is It Society's Fault?

Several books on male abusiveness have made the mistake of trying to explain it solely as a product of socialization—male expectations of privilege and power.[1] According to this view, for example, Juan was violent with Sandra because he was emulating the role model adopted by his father and the other violent men in his life or even those he had observed in the movies.

From my point of view, however, abusiveness can't be explained away by socialization. Too many men, socialized in the same culture as abusive men, remain nonabusive. Socialization has to be combined with psychological influences that precede it developmentally. I believe that most intimate abusiveness committed by men stems from the issues I've outlined in the previous two chapters: deep-seated feelings of powerlessness that have their origins in the man's early development. With a shaming, emotionally rejecting, or absent father, the boy is left in the arms of a mother who is only intermittently available but whom he perceives as all-powerful. He never recovers from the trauma.

For reasons that we have seen throughout this book, the impact of abuse and dysfunction in the family goes far beyond mere copying of abusive behaviors; it creates an environment for an entire constellation of thoughts and feelings known as the abusive personality. It is only after the personality originates that culture exerts its influence—and it exerts it unevenly on secure and insecure boys.

The boy whose early experiences have been dysfunctional, whose sense of personal identity has not been buttressed by his mother's warmth and his father's presence, is the one who is most susceptible to cast about desperately for aspects of the culture that will reaffirm or justify his abusiveness. Society can provide negative attitudes toward women and an acceptance of violence as a means of resolving conflict. Society helps mold aggression—it teaches the means, points to the target. Aggressive role models far outnumber creative ones. Power, control, and violence become the prevalent modes of resolving conflicts.

Nevertheless, attachment style, interest, and competing social influences take many boys away from the more aggressive mode. Boys who do have a secure attachment and identity take the cultural influences as they come, rejecting some outright, picking up parts of others. Their persona or social identity is a melange of many sources. It is for this reason that not every boy emulates Rambo, and most of those who do, do so only as part of a stage. They develop and move on.

Socialization doesn't affect all boys equally, and the deleterious influences of macho movie heroes and monomaniacal sports coaches dissipate when the boy has a close, warm role model at home who helps him sort through his daily supply of social junk mail. With the supportiveness of a close male relationship, men in our research samples were less likely to have abusive personalities and were also less likely to hold negative beliefs and hostile attitudes toward women.

The impact of socialization on individual men varies greatly. They hold dissimilar beliefs about women, have differing individual needs for personal power with them, and act in varied ways toward them. We have to remember that more than 70 percent of married women report that their husbands are nonviolent throughout their marriages. The adoption of the more negative aspects of any culture's legacy about women occurs more in men who have an early developmental flaw that results in the development of an abusive personality.

■ From Father to Son?

Abusiveness begins in the family of origin through the experience of shaming behaviors, direct experience of abusiveness from a parent, and insecure attachment with a mother who is herself frequently abused. Violence in the family, therefore, is the third key factor in the formation of the abusive personality. In Juan Carlos and Sandra's families, as with Ignacio, Rosa, and Oscar, the abuse seems to have passed from generation to generation as if it were genetically encoded.

Most likely, it was not. As we saw in Chapter 4, not all youngsters who have witnessed family violence or who have been abused themselves become assaultive. Psychologists have tried to determine the percentage of abused children who go on to become abusing spouses or parents, but the path is neither simple nor direct.

In his national survey data, sociologist Murray Straus found that boys who witnessed their parents attack one another were more than three times as likely to assault their wives or become the victims of their wives' violence than boys who had not experienced these family disturbances.[2] Straus's survey, however, simply reported an association between home life and assaultiveness. There might have been other potential causes for adult abusiveness, such as emotional support being unavailable to the boys or the fact that they had been struck by parents themselves. Also, for reasons we don't fully understand, some sons of abusive fathers become adamantly nonviolent, perhaps defining themselves in opposition to their hurtful parent. These confounding factors make it difficult to isolate the cause of spousal abuse from survey research.

Moreover, if we study adult abusers and trace the violence back into their childhoods, we are likely to find a history of brutality. But such methods do not allow us to trace all of the cases in which an abused child does not go on to be violent himself—the so-called false positives.

To correct for this problem, scientists investigating the transmission of family violence have, instead, followed groups of previously identified abused children for years as they matured into adulthood. They discovered that abused children do have higher subsequent rates of violent crime. Indeed, my colleague Steve Hart and I found the type of abuse in the family was strongly related to the types of crimes federal prisoners committed. Violent men had been physically abused, sex offenders sexually abused.[3]

We can draw two conclusions from these findings. The first is that firsthand abuse experiences or even the witnessing of abuse increases one's chances of becoming violent. The second is that the majority of abused children *do not* go on to become abusive themselves. This is not a contradiction. It simply means that modeling or observation has an influence on later life, but doesn't totally determine one's behavior. In the case of the cyclically assaultive man, for example, I believe that his father's shaming behavior and the boy's ambivalent attachment to his intermittently available mother, coupled with sex role socialization, all combine to produce abusiveness. As with a chemical formula, many ingredients are required to produce a specific result.

There are numerous other experiences that can break the chain of abusiveness from one generation to another. Many abused children may not have had the need or the adult opportunity to engage in violence. Others may have come under the influence of what we call protective factors—positive events that could mitigate against early negative experiences. One of these factors is having at least one supportive adult in an otherwise hostile early environment. Another is being in an emotionally supportive family as an adult. Involvement in psychotherapy as an adolescent or young adult is also helpful in breaking the cycle of violence. Still others have had their violence punished, ending its use as a behavioral strategy.[4]

However, negative factors may exert influence as well. The child may have learned passive strategies, such as "tuning out" the parent (learning to self-hypnotize or dissociate) or running away to deal with the violence. In fact, using aggression against an abusive parent is likely to be punished in the extreme, so the child may not consider that mode of behavior a viable option. Escape into television, music, or absorbing hobbies are other passive modes of dealing with an intolerable home situation.

■The Child's Emotional Experience During Violence

Abusers do not seem controllable. To the child observing or receiving the violence, they seem to have all the power. During an abusive incident, the child will endure aversive arousal—that uncomfortable state of tense, frenzied agitation that he feels must be blunted in order to survive. Just how he staves off the aversive arousal depends on his learning history. Either he will see the event that caused the arousal as controllable, or he won't.

In the latter case, if he cannot control what is occurring in his environment, he will try to reduce the tension any way he safely can—usually by escaping or withdrawing. Let's say, for example, that the abusive father's behavior triggers the aversive arousal. The father comes home late, drunk, yelling. He startles the kids and insults and threatens his wife. He starts smashing dishes and throwing table lamps and vases. Think back to the case of Ignacio.

In this case, the child is in no position to control his father's behavior. Maybe he tried once but learned that it was unwise, as the father trained his sights on him. He feels utterly powerless. (Interestingly, on the rare occasions that abuse victims do fight back, they are often amazed that their former tormentor is actually vulnerable. Ignacio, for example, could not believe that he had killed Oscar. Someone that powerful could not be dead.) In most cases, however, the child is left with few alternatives—since he is so overpowered.

The child might try retreating to his room. If that succeeds, he might escape further by listening to his Walkman to tune out his father's angry voice. But if that doesn't work, if the father won't let the child flee, if, as in Ignacio's case, he demands his undivided attention, his route to quiescence is blocked.

In this instance, the youngster would again be placed in the untenable state of learned helplessness. As I explained in Chapter 5, under these difficult circumstances, the child swallows his rage toward the perpetrator and experiences shame at his own impotence. This further undermines his sense of self.

When parental abuse is chronic, it wears down a child's defenses so that active strategies to reduce the negative feelings seem beyond his will. Many youngsters who grow up in abusive households learn passive withdrawal as a way to lessen the aversive arousal they feel. They retreat into other worlds—television, computers, music, books—and begin to inhabit those worlds exclusively. The body is still present in everyday reality, but the mind is somewhere else.

Another response to repeated trauma is dissociation: The individual learns to split his body from his mind. An incest victim, who cannot escape the attack, learns to "watch" her own victimization from a spot on the ceiling. She dispassionately sees her uncle performing sexual acts on her. When interviewed about her adult life of prostitution, she describes her tricks in the same dissociated manner. No feeling, no facial expression. "I was going down on him," she states matter-of-factly, "and the cops were cruisin' by." She has learned to cut off all feeling associated with her sexuality—that is, to self-hypnotize. The split was forced on her by the trauma of the early sexual violation. Some therapists refer to this as *psychic numbing*.

When these evasive tactics fail to reduce the pain, victims try more radical strategies such as running away, getting sick, or attempting suicide—anything to rid themselves of the queer feeling in the pit of the stomach.

■The Rewards of Anger

If, on the other hand, the child views the negative event as controllable, his aversive arousal will convert into feelings of rage. This prepares him to take action, and it overrides any other unacceptable emotions such as fear or guilt that might interfere. Indeed, his anger may give him a sense of control.[5] To borrow a phrase from Eric Fromm, anger converts impotence into omnipotence.[6] One's alienation and self-blame are transformed into feelings of power, conviction, and self-worth while the oppressor is vilified and becomes a worthy target for violence.

Anger is a highly self-reinforcing emotion that carries with it built-in rewards. Its expression can be intrinsically gratifying. It feels good to release the body's pent-up tension. According to psychologist Raymond Novaco, anger can also energize us and increase the vigor with which we act. That, in turn, can enhance our chances of being rewarded (in this case, with the termination of the aversive events). Anger advertises one's potency, expressiveness, and determination. To the extent that these qualities are thought to be part of one's sex role, the expression of anger enhances one's self image. For example, getting angry may be consistent with a man's notion of manliness.

Anger also short-circuits anxious feelings of vulnerability. Since the cultivation of invulnerability is the cornerstone of male socialization, for a man it is less distressing to be angry than to feel afraid. Anger and fear are more closely related than most people realize, however. I remember hearing a veteran of D-Day describe his feelings as the Allied troops were huddling in the boats off Normandy, readying themselves to assault the German army. They experienced abject fear, but they stormed the shore, guns blazing, anyway. That's what they'd been trained to do—to act despite fear. Men are taught from birth that only wimps show fear.

If a man learns this lesson really well, he gets to the point where he doesn't even detect fear at low levels, not in everyday circumstances and not about issues like being separated from his wife. What he feels instead is irritation and anger. For some men, to be in an intimate relationship at all inevitably generates fear, shame, and rejection—and anger as a cover—but the anger is more compatible with action. Abusive men will use anger to cover the painful feelings of fear and rejection associated with their early ambivalent or fearful attachment in a way that's consonant with their sex roles and their view of manliness. Fearful attachment becomes angry attachment. Anger also externalizes conflict by directing attention outward; by blaming the other, we need never feel shame or guilt. Most abusive men have buried these unacceptable feelings very deeply, using anger as their shovel.

All of these aspects of anger are shaped by culture. Men are programmed to ignore their fear and act anyway—to be *agentic*. When situations seem to be whirling out of control, men tend to react with anger and action. However, the form that emotion takes, its target (a woman, another man, or oneself), and its means of expression (verbal sarcasm, physical abuse) vary enormously from man to man. In these ways, the emotional response to provocation is learned and a habit of anger sustained.

Lenny, the psychopath we met in Chapter 2, taught himself the habit of violence. During group treatment, he reported his first attempt to stop aggression directed toward him by fighting back.

One day, when he was coming home from school, some bigger boys—the neighborhood bullies—chased him and picked a fight. That had happened before, and in most instances Lenny was able to outrun them. But twice they had caught him and beaten him up.

That day, however, he was ready. He had been practicing fighting skills with his older brother. When one of his tormentors approached, Lenny didn't hesitate. He punched him hard in the face, then kicked him in the groin. The boy fell to the ground. Lenny kicked him senseless.

He felt great, he recalled later, "like I was king of the world, or somethin'." That night, he practiced fighting even harder. Lenny's habitual way of dealing with bullies was born. Soon this tactic was generalized to anyone who disagreed with him.

Gerald Patterson and his colleagues at the Oregon Learning Center in Eugene have studied aggressive boys in detail. In one investigation, they observed boys like Lenny who were initially passive. Some stayed out of trouble by avoiding others. They remained nonaggressive. Others were forced into battle like Lenny. Many lost, got beaten up, and remained submissive. Others occasionally succeeded in halting the attack by fighting back.

Something strange happened to the latter group. They not only learned to use aggression as a defensive tactic, but they went on the offense, looking for fights. Where once they had been avoidant, they became predatory. This trial-and-error learning gradually shapes behavior and gets it to take the narrow form we call habitual. The action becomes fixed and rigid as the individual's repertoire for problem solving atrophies to this narrow band. All conflicts lead automatically and quickly to the learned habit—anger and the threat of aggression.[7]

Aggression is designed to control and change people. If the

aggressor yells, stomps, and screams, if he threatens bodily harm and then makes good on his threat, others fall quickly into line. If the violence rids the aggressor of his tension states by cathartic discharge or changing the actions of the "offending" person, then the violence is rewarded. The abusive man uses aggression to control the degree of intimacy in a relationship. If he is successful, the habit of violence soon becomes entrenched.

■The Mother's Reaction

Some contradiction and ambivalence is inevitable in an abused mother's behavior. Psychologist David Winter speculates that mothers in patriarchal societies act ambivalently toward male children as an act of retaliation against men, specifically against the child's father and her own father. This retaliation is most likely in societies where there is great differentiation of the sexes and women are suppressed and restricted by men. The ensuing anger felt by women infuses their relationship with their own son, interspersing nurturance with rejection.[8]

From my experience, if a boy's father is rejecting and abusive, the boy is affected in many ways. Not only may he model the father's actions or feel hurt by the father's rejection, but the father's behavior will also impact on the boy's mother and influence her relationship with her son. It is for this reason that specific maternal behaviors, even if they may generate psychological damage to the son, cannot be blamed on the mother. She may be a link in the tortuous chain of a dysfunctional family. Her own power needs, indirect rage, and ambivalence toward her son may be generated by an intermittently abusive relationship with her husband, a society that disempowers her, or both.

The psychology of abusiveness interacts with socially sanctioned role models. Abusiveness gets its start in the family of origin through the experience of shaming behaviors, direct experience of violence from a parent, and insecure attachment with a mother who herself is frequently abused. The shaming experiences by themselves create a person who rejects any criticism, angers easily, and blames others for the frequent anger he feels. He cannot and does not understand his rage and frequent depression as aspects of his own personality.

The anger and blaming serve to avoid the excruciating experience of shame. Both anger and blame are in the service of the ego—they keep it intact and protect its integrity. After all, it has been assailed at its most vulnerable stage and is now quite guarded. Both anger and blame see to that.

The acting out of abusiveness is facilitated by having had an abusive role model at home. Most fathers who shamed their sons also abused them or their wives. The shaming experience and the violent role model usually go hand in hand—one usually cannot be separated from the other.

8 The Assaultive Man as an Adolescent

PAUL THOMPSON CAME TO GROUP AT THE AGE OF NINETEEN. He hadn't completed high school yet. Although he admitted to having hit girlfriends since he was about thirteen, his first serious abusive incident occurred at seventeen. He had been at a party, drinking and dancing. There were some drugs. He was with his first steady girlfriend—the relationship had lasted more than three weeks. They had gotten into an argument, although he couldn't remember much about it. He walked out of the party, and Brenda came after him, shouting, "Don't go." He wheeled around and punched her. One of her girlfriends called the cops, and eventually the court referred him to me.

Paul was still living with his parents. When I spoke briefly to his mother, she said, "He's incorrigible. We don't know what to do with him. He's been a problem child ever since he was seven." She talked about him breaking things, having a temper, being rebellious.

When I interviewed Paul, I thought he might have some neurological problems. He had been diagnosed with an attention deficit disorder. He had strange body language. He always sat in the corner of the room, his head turned toward the wall, his body sort of slumped away. When I spoke to him, he would look up at me briefly, then avert his eyes again.

According to Paul, the main problem in his life was his mother. He couldn't get along with her. But the strange thing about Mrs. Thompson was that she wouldn't let me interview her. She told me on the phone that she hoped we could "fix" her son, but then never assisted us by shedding light on the problem.

Paul showed up for the first four weeks of group then dropped out for two. When he came back, he said he had spent those fourteen days in bed. He hadn't left his room. This type of severe withdrawal usually indicates an anxiety about attack from some vague, unspecified outside force.

Paul talked about hitting his other girlfriends. They would leave him then and go back to their parents. He had all the potential of being a serial abuser, including diminished awareness. When I asked him why he had assaulted the girls, he simply said, "They got in my face." That was the limit of what he could describe.

With adults, cyclical battering emerges as the man feels vulnerable in an ongoing relationship. The repetitive buildup of violence is directed against one woman. That's the hallmark of a couple old enough to stay in a long-term relationship. But if abuse occurs when teens like Paul and Brenda are dating, the relationship usually ends. As an adolescent, the boy will blow out his rage and the girl will leave. He will then denigrate and dismiss her. "She was a bitch," he'll say. "She was a problem. Boy, am I ever glad I got rid of her." And he goes on to the next girl.

The statistics on dating violence are frightening: The rates are much higher than for domestic abuse, with as many as 40 to 50 percent of dating couples experiencing some sort of violence.[1] Late adolescence is the peak age for nonintimate violence in men. The average age of homicide perpetrators is eighteen.[2] Perhaps this is caused by a combination of hormones and other factors including the rebellion or tension related to leaving home and establishing oneself for the first time. For the chronically assaultive man, however, it may be activated by a confluence of maturing violent impulses.

■ The Obscured Emergence of an Abuser

Imagine a man with the type of upbringing described in the last several chapters. He enters his teens angry but doesn't know why. Everybody else writes it off to teenage angst or hormones. He feels distanced from his family but figures that every other teenager does, too. The MTV culture supports him in this belief. Parents are almost universally portrayed as insensitive, rule-obsessed, and unhip. He believes that if he can only achieve the teenage state of cool, he will mask his inner shame. What's more, since adolescence is notorious for identity problems, his quests do not appear atypical.

His growing obsession with girls is also written off as "a phase he's going through." What teenaged boy isn't interested in girls? Parents usually worry only when their sons aren't interested. Even his stormy relationships with girlfriends are easily ignored. Teenagers are famous for falling in love frequently and then breaking up. It's one of the trademarks of being an adolescent.

The difference is that for securely based youths, this truly is just a phase. The teenage years—the very age at which most boys get their first taste of intimate attachment—are notable for identity issues. Psychologist Erik Erikson talks about the central crisis of adolescence as identity versus role diffusion.[3] But if we're focusing on a boy who is carrying with him earlier identity problems such as the inability to trust or the feeling of being inferior, these color and shape his development into adolescence and adulthood. For the emergent assaultive man who is saddled with these earlier deficits and unresolved conflicts, the problem of counterbalancing identity and intimacy is the beginning of a life-long preoccupation.

The problem is further confounded for teenage boys. Typically, their only adult male contacts are their fathers and teachers or sports coaches. If their fathers are already emotionally withdrawn or abusive, that doesn't leave much in the way of support. Sports coaches are famous for teaching boys to ignore their feelings and soldier on: "When the going gets tough, the tough get going." There no help here in sorting out inner states of dread or confusion. The message is simply to ignore the inner aspect of experience and focus on the outer world. This practiced dismissal of inner emotional experience will create special problems for a boy whose subjective world is fraught with anxiety, depression, and anger.

The external focus often serves escape functions for tormented boys. They throw themselves into sports, music, or whatever grabs their interest. Again, the culture values the discipline of spending hours on the basketball court or hockey rink practicing shooting. Boys who want to wall themselves off in their rooms and rehearse their guitar riffs generally are left alone with a sense of relief on the part of their parents. These activities lead to perfected skills but also to emotional withdrawal. A biography of rock guitarist Eric Clapton shows how hours of practicing blues guitar provided escape for a vulnerable boy who had discovered his "parents" were really his grandparents and that he had been abandoned by his biological parents.[4] The escape is typically short-lived. Clapton eventually succumbed to (and recovered from) both drug and alcohol addictions.

The primitive defenses learned during infancy come into play now. These include tendencies to project blame outward and to split women into Madonnas and whores. The first of these, the projection of blame, is again consistent with male socialization. Regrets and apologies hinder achievement, determination, and single-minded pursuits of excellence. What if Elvis had taken to heart his rude put-down by the Grand Ole Opry? Would he have become the king of rock and roll? Of course not. Every man of achievement has had to develop some hubris at one point or another in his career.

How then to separate this habit of blaming in the dog-eat-dog outside world from the boy's ability to hear and empathize at home? For every man, this is a contradiction that must be gradually resolved if he wants to survive in the world and also be intimate. For someone whose tendency is to project blame in order to avoid shame, this balancing act is almost impossible. Society again colludes with early upbringing to generate a problem child in the body of a man.

■ Emergent Sexuality and Misogyny

The primitive defense of splitting is also socially reinforced during adolescence. The preabusive boy grows up with two unconscious schematas for women: templates of an erstwhile accommodating mother and a frustrating bitch both reside in his mind. He has a Manichean view of womanhood, splitting women into rigid good and evil categories. Again his culture encourages him to put every girl or woman he meets into one of these categories. Every school has "good girls" and "bad girls" and every boy knows who they are. Having a sexually loose girlfriend is humiliating. At the same time, being sexually promiscuous is a sign of manhood to many boys.

The old double standard is probably a vestige of church thinking. After all, the history of misogyny in the church, as we noted in Chapter 4, is as extensive as the history of religion itself. Women, easily seduced by devils, are more susceptible than men to diabolical influence. Women, therefore, require punishment for correction. Old beliefs die hard. As I pointed out earlier, slasher films, which make up a large part of teenage boys' movie-watching repertoires, along with macho, violent action films, typically have a bad girl character who is gruesomely murdered. The explicit message: She was bad, she messed around, she had it coming. This badness represents a projection of the bad side of oneself onto women, a bad side that is sexual, impulsive, and unreliable. The whore becomes the recipient of these split-off projected impulses.

Boys who are potentially abusive pick up on these cultural messages differently than those who are not. Indeed, they might be more likely to look for negative messages about women in society. Personality variables can influence what we take from the culture. Research has shown that as early as age nineteen, college students with the potential for abusive personalities have more negative attitudes and hostility toward women than those without this potential.

For example, my graduate student Andrew Starzomski and I tested the way young men think about intimate events in a unique investigation.[5] Instead of studying batterers, we evaluated middle-class university students. Although these boys were only twenty years old, almost all had been in serious intimate relationships. First they filled out many of the same questionnaires we use with batterers to identify whether they had the tendency to become abusers. Then we gave them a strange test.

After listening to audiotapes of couples in conflict, they answered a questionnaire that assessed what they thought about the events that they had just overheard. To what cause was an act attributed? If a future conflict occurred, would the persons involved act the same way? Did they behave purposefully—to hurt or spite the other? We replayed specific words or actions from the original context and asked the boys why the man or woman reacted the way he or she did.

We assessed these boys using our psychological test batteries and found that the young men in our study who exhibited a higher tendency to have abusive personalities were also more likely to blame the woman for the conflict and to see her actions as intended to hurt her boyfriend. They also thought she would continue to do these things in the future. When these boys were played snippets of conflicted couples interacting and asked what caused the problem, they always ticked off the box indicating the woman. They perceived her actions differently than did the boys who were not inclined to abusiveness.

What's more, the potentially abusive boys saw this as a stable feature of their own relationships. "She's the cause and this won't change." In this sense, their way of viewing relationships fueled and maintained their intimate rage. The blaming mindset kept the anger level high. And conversely, the thoughts and feelings of the abusive man reinforce each other. Some of the college men we assessed are the abusive husbands of the future.

The abusive teenage boy quickly learns to use the readymade categories of "good girl" and "bad girl" since they fit his split inner representations. His mom and sister, of course, are Madonnas. They can't possibly have sex. Then there's the problem of his girlfriend. He wants to sleep with her but he wants to respect her, too. He needs sex but he also needs to control her sexuality. Any notion of her as a free-spirited sexual person precludes the latter. If he puts her in a Madonna category, he restricts his own sexuality toward her. If he puts her in the whore category, he cannot bring himself to trust her, and his jealousy becomes uncontrollable. He quickly starts sending her confusing mixed messages about his desires. He is unclear about what he himself wants.

Somehow, out of this balancing act, he will try to preserve the Madonna while bedding the whore. Usually, he fails at this, slipping off the tightrope on one side or the other. He either gets too sexually wild with his girlfriend and then can't conceive of being vulnerable and committed to "someone like that," or he restricts his own response so much that the vital energy of the relationship dries up. In either case, the undertow of one schemata or the other drags him under.

When the inevitable occurs, and the relationship hits the wall, it reinforces his concept of Madonnas and whores. If the boy acts out abusively, he typically sees his girlfriend as the cause of his behavior. As he lurches from one failed relationship to the next because of his own impossible demands, he blames the failures on the woman. At first he blames one woman, then another, and eventually he blames women in general. This process is the mid-wife at the birth of misogyny.

Indeed, the abusive teen draws upon misogyny in the culture to facilitate and reinforce his views. These negative attitudes toward women are not, in themselves, a first cause of his behavior. Rather, they are by-products of that abusiveness, which eventually serve both to justify and to perpetuate it. In this sense, the culture fosters abusiveness, but not for all men equally. Those who are psychologically predisposed adopt misogyny as a rationalization for their behavior toward women. Other men resist both the abusive behavior and the misogyny.

The prototypes for abusiveness, which we described in the previous chapters, manifest themselves in the teenage years, in a culture that colludes in their development. The way we raise boys in this society does nothing to correct tendencies toward maintaining an abusive personality in adulthood. If anything, such a personality and the attitudinal baggage that it carries are reinforced by the culture's view of women.

In our research, the abusive personality is highly correlated with holding negative views of women and experiencing hostile mind-sets or attitudes. The abusive personality believes, "Women are out to get me." It is for this reason that purely cultural explanations of male violence and misogyny are incomplete. Not all boys adopt the negative attitudes that the culture holds toward women. The boy's psychology influences his tendency to embrace them or not. Abusive boys look to the culture for beliefs to rationalize their preexisting rage toward women. They find them all too easily.

Many of these boys grew up with unrewarding attachment, and their rage simmers just below the surface. Their fears of abandonment become reshaped with sexual content and emerge as intense sexual jealousy. In my research, the men who had the highest scores for fearful attachment also had the highest scores for jealousy.[6] In a narrower, sexual sense, jealousy is the terror of abandonment, the terror of losing one's mother, which, in time, transmogrifies into the terror of losing one's lover.

In order to act in the world—to be agentic—some men believe that one must be fearless (as fear can hamper action), insensitive (as sensitivity can impede action), egocentric (as egocentricity convinces one of the rightness of one's intended action), and invulnerable (as insecurity can undermine action). But invulnerability requires a gradual dulling of those emotions that are inconsistent with agency: anxiety, dependency, and fear. These "weaker emotions" are converted and subsumed by role-consistent actions: anger and sexual predation.

As a result, the abusive teenager's anger begins to override his anxiety and dependency. His felt need for attachment is converted into "horniness" in the language he uses in communicating with other boys and in his own self-talk. Feelings such as loneliness disappear from his emotional lexicon and are reborn as sexual longing. Again, a compelling example of this is the blues. Here, depression over loss is expressed as a moan or wail, and the language of loss is of a sexual object. "My little dough roller be gone," sings Robert Johnson.

The range of emotional states is narrowed, constricted, and funneled into culturally acceptable forms. These emotions have a robust and complex street vocabulary with a variety of vulgar expressions. He says, "I need to get laid," not "I am lonely and miss contact." The sexual act involves attachment, connection, verbal and emotional sharing, but these aspects are downplayed.

The abusive personality originates early in the man's developmental history, then it repeatedly re-creates itself during adolescence, aided and abetted by the ambient culture. With each re-creation, the personality becomes more fixed, more intransigent, more intractable.

9 The Borderline Male: The Cycle of Fear and Rage

THE PATTERN THAT I HAVE CALLED THE ABUSIVE PERSONALITY will not occur in exactly the same fashion in every cyclically abusive man. It is better thought of as a matrix in which some individual differences are inevitable. Nevertheless, the abiding elements (anger, jealousy, blaming, recurring moods, and trauma symptoms) are generally present in all cyclical abusers. So too are the forms of abusiveness. The two most frequent are emotional abuse and domination/control. Rarer is physical battering, and least common of all is sexual assault. But when these latter do occur, they are almost always accompanied by the first. The consistencies in the profiles of cyclically abusive men are striking.

The Borderline Personality Connection

From the beginnings of recorded medical and literary history, writers have recognized the coexistence within certain individuals of intense and divergent moods such as euphoria, irritability, and depression. Both Homer and Hippocrates described with great vividness the related character of impulsive anger, mania, and melancholia, noting the erratic variations among these "spells" and the personalities likely to be affected by them.

In 1987, at a jungle hotel outside Puerto Vallarta, I found a psychiatric diagnosis that matched my own observations of and research into this type of personality. I had taken along a copy of psychiatrist John Gunderson's book *Borderline Personality Disorder*[1] as part of my not-so-light holiday reading. In it, I made a startling discovery: A borderline personality experiences three dramatically different phases that produce sudden shifts in his world view—dysphoric stalemate, angry outburst, and aloneness-anxiety. Preoccupations, perspectives on intimate relationships, emotions, and behavior fluctuate from one phase to the next, leading to *a repetitive or cyclical personality*. Could the cyclical wife assaulters I'd been studying suffer from borderline personality disorder?

Borderline personality is a clinical category developed in the psychiatric literature for people who are neither psychotic nor neurotic. Indeed, the term originally referred to people who existed on the border between these two disorders. Borderlines do not confuse themselves with another person, the way that psychotic people might, but they have a split in their self-perceptions. Part of themselves just cannot be fit or integrated with other parts. Again, I wondered if this split might be related to the Dr. Jekyll and Mr. Hyde descriptions given by the wives of cyclically abusive men.

In the past, psychiatrists had focused on women with borderline personalities, simply because the bulk of their clinical outpatients were female. Borderline women seek help more easily; borderline men act out and get into trouble. I have come to believe that some of these troubled men—those who are cyclically abusive—wound up in our groups and research studies. (The diagnosis of borderline personality, however, would not apply to abusers who are psychopathic or to the overcontrolled wife assaulters.)

■   ■   ■

Psychiatrist Otto Kernberg estimates that 11 to 15 percent of the general population exhibit the symptoms of borderline personality organization; of these, only 10 to 25 percent manifest signs of the more severe version, borderline personality disorder.[2] A personality type becomes a disorder when it is so fixed and rigid as to cause the person interminable difficulties. People afflicted with a disorder literally cannot escape themselves. Clearly, though, even the less severe forms are problematic, and the point at which a personality type becomes a disorder is somewhat arbitrary.

The essential defining criteria for borderline personality, in order of importance, are: a proclivity for intense, unstable interpersonal relationships characterized by intermittent undermining of the significant other, manipulation, and masked dependency; an unstable sense of self with intolerance of being alone and abandonment anxiety; and intense anger, demandingness, and impulsivity, usually tied to substance abuse or promiscuity.

According to Gunderson, one of the essential features of the borderline personality is that the individual experiences repeated dissatisfactions with whomever he is attached. Moreover, he changes predictably over time. These phases sounded to me very much like those of the cycle of violence that Lenore Walker's women respondents described and also like what I had observed among my clients.[3] It was as though one could be mapped onto the other.

Phase one consists of an internal buildup of tension—what Gunderson calls a "dysphoric stalemate" in relationships. The individual feels depressed and irritable and doesn't know how to verbalize the psychic discomfort. He finds himself in a downward spiral of bad feelings. He desperately needs soothing and intimate connection, but is unable to recognize this or express it.

The problem is exacerbated by the fact that the borderline personality literally needs the intimate other to help sustain his sense of self-integrity. The glue of selfhood, which bonds strongly for most people, repeatedly dilutes for the borderline. He begins to feel, every now and then, as if he will "fly apart" (*identity diffusion*), and a strange anxiety overcomes him. He experiences a growing sense of fear and unreality. His wife appears not to understand or love him, and she becomes the focus of his displeasure.

Of course, during this phase, the borderline becomes increasingly tense and unlovable. He begins to push his intimate partner away. Yet, underneath the building irritability and rageful accusations, there exists an intense demandingness, probably impossible for the other person to meet. This first stage matches the tension building phase of the abuse cycle.

According to Gunderson, the unexpressed hostility builds until the borderline erupts in phase two, an angry outburst, which corresponds with the abusive explosions we have seen. If the rage drives away the significant other, phase three (aloneness-anxiety) begins. The borderline engages in desperate attempts to ward off the feeling of aloneness. Binge drinking, drugs, and promiscuity occur most frequently during this third phase.

The contrition phase of the abuse cycle might also fit this third category. The man promises anything to get his woman back—to ward off the subjective experience of aloneness. She, who was recently so despicable to him, is now essential. Once at her throat, he is now at her knees. These behaviors persist until the woman has tentatively returned. Gradually, the special appeasement behavior subsides, and the cycle eventually repeats.

Psychologist Theodore Millon has traced the historical antecedents of the current borderline label back to the seventeenth century, when the emphasis was on the impulsive and erratic moods of the individual. Millon saw the "depth and variability of moods" as the central feature of borderlines. These are "unpredictable and appear prompted less by external events than by internal factors."[4]

The predisposition to become a borderline personality is in place from early childhood and is noticeable from repeated failures at coping, which Millon describes as a merry-go-round of recurring disturbances with no evidence of learning from mistakes. As he puts it, "The borderline patient goes round in circles, covering the same ground as before, getting nowhere, and then starting all over again."[5]

Borderlines experience transient periods in which they exhibit irrational impulses. "Fears and urges that derive from an obscure inner source take over and engulf them in an ocean of primitive anxieties and behaviors."[6] Unable to understand the source of their own malaise, they may engage in erratic and hostile behavior or embark on "wild and chaotic sprees" that they can barely remember later. These episodes of emotional discharge serve as a release valve for mounting internal pressures.

For these reasons, borderlines have checkered work and school histories. They tend to exhibit extreme unevenness in fulfilling normal social functions and responsibilities.

Millon writes that the borderline experience is typified by "intense, variable moods and irregular energy levels, both of which appear to be unrelated to external events." These individuals endure a deep fear of separation and loss. They require considerable reassurance in order to maintain equilibrium. But they are also conflicted about their need for the other. "Strong ambivalent feelings, such as love, anger, and guilt are often felt toward those upon whom there is dependence."[7]

According to the *Diagnostic and Statistical Manual* (DSM-IV), the psychological and psychiatric community's diagnostic bible, at least three of the following criteria must be present to a notable degree in order for an individual to be diagnosed with borderline personality disorder:

1. Recurring periods of dejection and apathy interspersed with spells of anger, anxiety, or euphoria.

2. Wavering energy levels and irregular sleep-wake cycles.

3. Repetitive self-destructive thoughts. The borderline redeems moody behavior by derogating himself.

4. A preoccupation with securing affection and maintaining emotional support. The borderline reacts intensely to separation and reports a haunting fear of isolation and loss.

5. Conflicting emotions toward others, notably love, rage, and guilt.

With the exception of the third criterion, these all seem consistent with cyclically abusive men. And if you changed that guideline to read, "The borderline redeems moody behavior by derogating a *significant other*," you would have a perfect description of the wife assaulters I have been studying.

Borderlines have considerable difficulty maintaining a stable sense of who they are and therefore lack purpose or direction in their lives. Their self-definition depends strongly on their surrounding social group. Other consequences of their unstable identities are a tendency to become exceedingly dependent on others and a need for protection and reassurance. Borderlines are inordinately vulnerable to separation from their external sources of support. They suffer from intense abandonment anxiety, dreading potential loss while chronically anticipating it, "seeing it happening, when in fact it is not."[8]

Millon explains that since most borderlines devalue their self-worth, they have trouble believing that others—especially those upon whom they depend—think well of them. As a result, they are terrified that others will belittle and abandon them. "With so unstable a foundation of self-esteem, and lacking the means for an autonomous existence," he writes, "borderlines remain constantly on edge, prone to the anxiety of separation and ripe for anticipating inevitable desertion." Anything that might arouse these fears may activate "idealization, self-abnegation, and attention-gaining acts of self destruction or, conversely, self-assertion and impulsive anger."[9]

Matters are bad enough for borderlines given their identity diffusion and separation anxieties, but they are also in intense conflict regarding dependency. In their quest for self-identity as children and adolescents, many have been abused and shamed, subjected to ridicule and isolation, resulting in feelings of distrust and anger toward others. Borderlines cannot help but be ambivalently anxious. Given their past, they know they can never entirely trust others nor fully hope to gain the security and affection they need.

Moreover, borderlines experience intense anger toward those upon whom they depend, not only because their dependency shames them and exposes their weakness, but also because of the others' power in having "forced" them to yield and acquiesce. This very resentment becomes a threat in itself.

When I read Millon's description, I detected the personality origins of controlling behaviors and masked dependencies in cyclically abusive men. But these individuals hide those underlying feelings with the tendency to act out, to aggress, to vilify the other as a release from these tensions and a reaction against them. If a borderline man can blame his wife for his vague and semiconscious personal deficiencies, he won't have to face them in himself. That would undermine his carefully crafted masculine persona.

Borderlines blame their partners when things go wrong in intimate relationships. And things are always going wrong, because they set impossible standards and double-binds for others. As their tension mounts, the need for perfect control in an imperfect world generates inevitable failure. People are fallible. One man would inspect the house after his wife did the chores, running his finger under the refrigerator, looking for dust. Eventually, he found some. Then a two-hour harangue would ensue in which he screamed at her about her lousy housekeeping. This personality profile creates an environment in which relationship conflict and abuse are inevitable.

Other aspects of the borderline personality correspond with that of the cyclic abuser. Psychiatrist Bessel van der Kolk and his colleagues, for example, found that early trauma and abuse are more frequent in the histories of adult borderlines than in other clinical groups.[10] Moreover, excessive separations, losses, or disruptions were also more likely in the lives of borderline patients and federal prisoners convicted of crimes of violence. This was especially true for those convicted of family violence. Childhood trauma coupled with separations such as these almost always involves attachment disruptions for the child.

Van der Kolk suggests that physical abuse produces long-term difficulties in modulating emotion and aggression and gives some hints as to the gender origins of chronic anger in males. The emotional problems appear as a numbing or constriction that includes the inability to recognize and make use of emotional reactions. This is followed by extreme arousal with a very strong pulse, sometimes visible as a bulging neck vein, speedy actions, sweating, and aggressive outbursts.

The form the aggression takes seems to be influenced by sex roles. Abused boys identify with the aggressor and subsequently act out, whereas abused girls turn to self-destructive acts.[11] Psychologist Cathy S. Widom also found that childhood victimization (by physical abuse) increased overall risk for violent offending, particularly for males.[12] Since many early studies of borderlines were based on female psychiatric patients, the male acting out of aggression was often overlooked.

■ Testing for Borderline Personality Organization

These descriptions of borderline personality organization sounded exactly like the cyclically abusive husbands of the battered women I have known. It was only the prevailing opinion of the time that prevented family violence researchers from seeking a personality explanation for these men. The emphasis, then, was on societally induced "male violence" in general and not on the personality profiles of particular men.

In 1989, I started to test wife assaulters for borderline personality organization. The instrument I used, devised by a group of psychiatrists lead by Dr. John Oldham, measured three aspects of this profile: identity diffusion (an unstable self-concept), primitive defenses (splitting, projection, and denial), and lapses in reality testing (not knowing sometimes whether sensations come from outside or within).[13] Borderlines typically experienced a lot of ambivalence (dependency and hostility) toward intimates and an equal measure of expressed anger. The Oldham scale was a way of translating the inner experience of these men into a measurable score on a self-report scale.

The identity diffusion subscale, for example, measures "a poorly integrated sense of self . . . reflected in a subjective experience of chronic emptiness, or in contradictory perceptions of the self, contradictory behavior that cannot be integrated in an emotionally meaningful way."[14] This is manifested through difficulties in describing the self, uncertainty about career or goals, incongruous behaviors, and instabilities in intimate relationships.

Items on the test that reflected identity diffusion included: "I see myself in totally different ways at different times," "I find it hard to describe myself," "It is hard for me to be sure about what others think of me, even people who have known me very well." All of these items assess an insecurity or uncertainty about the self.

Another item, "I feel empty inside," taps into a second important dimension, a sense of inner oblivion. I wondered if someone who is insecure and who struggled against a gnawing sense of emptiness would experience greater anxieties about intimacy. Would he have higher expectations of his partner, ultimately demanding that the relationship fill the internal void? Another item reads, "I feel that I'm a different person at home compared to how I am at work or school." This reveals several other central themes of abusiveness: The abuse is private, and the man appears quite differently to his wife than his workmates—the Jekyll and Hyde motif.

The second of Oldham's subscales, called primitive defenses, measures splitting, projection, and denial (see Chapter 6). With splitting, the borderline either idealizes or devalues his significant other. This corresponds to how batterers flip-flop from one week to the next in describing their wives. "I act in ways that strike others as unpredictable or erratic," or "I tend to feel things in a somewhat extreme way, experiencing either great joy or intense despair."

Projection means that the individual perceives in the intimate other those aspects that he can't face in himself. He projects them onto the other. Some items measuring projection included: "People tend to respond to me by either overwhelming me with love or abandoning me."

This instrument also measures primitive denial. When in this state, borderlines are aware that "their perceptions, thoughts and feelings about themselves . . . are opposite to those they may have at other times, but this awareness has no emotional relevance for them."[15] That is, the split itself is denied. The item "I act in ways that strike others as unpredictable and erratic" addresses this dimension. While many of us may sense contradictions in ourselves, this alone will not generate a high score on the Oldham scale. Only a cumulative agreement with a variety of such items qualifies one as a borderline.

The two items most strongly associated with borderline personality measure themes of trust and abandonment: "It is hard for me to trust people because they so often turn against me or abandon me," and "People tend to respond to me by either overwhelming me with love or abandoning me." The scale acknowledges fear of abandonment, another characteristic of abusive men.

The final portion of this instrument is called reality testing. To a certain extent, this questionnaire defines borderlines as distinct from psychotics. While the latter constantly experience difficulty with reality testing, the former have only "transient psychotic states," during which they have difficulty distinguishing internally originating perceptions from those that arise externally. Items in the reality testing portion include statements such as "I can't tell whether certain physical sensations I'm having are real or whether I am imagining them."

Other features of reality testing involve the inability to differentiate the self from the nonself. Items assessing this issue include

"I've had relationships in which I couldn't tell whether I or the other person was thinking or feeling something." Test subjects are also asked to evaluate their behavior in terms of social criteria of reality ("Somehow, I never know how to conduct myself with people").

I was interested in how scores on this borderline dimension related to abusiveness. The next step in the research was to directly measure these scores and relate them to other aspects of abusiveness. Did this disorder carry with it associated features such as anger, jealousy, and violence? These are the feelings and perceptions that set the stage for someone to be abusive. The higher the correlation, the more strongly associated are the two measures. With our men, we would have to make the case for cause (personality) and effect (abusiveness) on theoretical grounds. That is, I would argue that all the evidence points toward personality being formed early in life, while the behavior doesn't occur until adolescence or adulthood.

We also threw another measure into our assessment package almost as an afterthought: the Trauma Symptom Checklist (see Chapter 4), in which respondents report the frequency with which they experience certain post-traumatic stress symptoms.[16] We also used a test to measure fearful attachment (see Chapter 6) and the Conflict Tactics Scale to assess the level of family violence.

After I had chosen the assessment instruments, my next step was to have men who were in treatment for wife assault complete the questionnaires. I approached therapists in two treatment programs, one dealing almost exclusively with court-mandated men and another with self-referred men. The first group had been convicted of wife assault and were sent to treatment as a condition of their probation. Their motivation to participate in treatment and to complete psychological tests was mixed at best. The self-referred men had shown up largely at the behest of their wives, who had promised to leave if they didn't get treatment for their abusiveness. We came to call these men "wife-mandated."

I assessed the referred men for suitability for treatment by interviewing them in an old family court building. I clearly remember some of the less-motivated men. One sat nervously in the waiting room dressed in a tank top and cut-offs. When I started the interview he squirmed and seethed at me disdainfully. After a few factual questions, I said, "Tell me what happened the time you were charged."

He looked at me out of the corner of his eye and spat out, "None of your fuckin' business." Treatment for him, I thought, was going to be an uphill struggle. Usually the dialogue goes something like:

"We were having an argument."

"What about?"

"Can't remember." Or, "We were both drunk. I must have pushed her. She called the cops."

The men made up lots of excuses in their interviews:

"She was pretty upset at the time, and said a lot of stuff that she later tried to take back."

"Her sister came to court and lied. She never did like me."

"My lawyer told me to plead guilty. He said it would be over faster."

Clearly these were not men who were going to be forthcoming on psychological questionnaires.

The self-referred men were easier in some ways. They had at least acknowledged that they had a problem. On the other hand, they often seemed more maladjusted than the court-referred men, angrier, more jealous, and more depressed.

At first my cotherapists wouldn't agree to mandatory assessment of the men. They felt it was unethical to force them to complete questionnaires. So we made sure to let them know that the testing was voluntary. Under these circumstances, unfortunately, only about half completed the tests. They would take them home reluctantly but then "forget" to fill them out, saying that the kids spilled soup on them or the dog ate them.

Eventually, I was able to convince my colleagues that if we were going to do the research properly, we would have to make the assessments mandatory.[17] Only in this way would we get everyone referred to the program filling out the questionnaires instead of a self-selected few. However, if we were going to tell the men that the assessment was mandatory, we would have to really use it and give them some feedback on their test scores.

There were still other problems. How could we be sure the men were filling out the questionnaires honestly? Was it possible for them to see through the test and answer in a socially desirable way—that is, to make themselves look good in our eyes? Fortunately, we could measure just how much respondents were faking good answers and mathematically cleanse their scores of these responses.[18]

By discerning what the men were embellishing most about themselves or, conversely, what they were hiding, we got a snapshot of their conscience and their sense of guilt and shame. After all, people only deny those aspects of themselves that they suspect are unacceptable to others.

For example, self-referred men underreported their high levels of anxiety, sleep disturbances, and depression. We surmised that since these were so prevalent, the men might have felt unmanly admitting it. Court-referred men tended to idealize their parents. In general, the men tried to hide their hostile outlook, their tendency to let their anger out, and their emotional and physical abusiveness. They had an even harder time admitting anger than abusiveness.

For about a year, the self-reports of clients in the treatment groups came trickling in. It was hard work. Not only were many of the men unreceptive, but many of their partners were hard to find. Some had left after the violence, others wanted nothing to do with the men, their treatment, or some psychologists with questionnaires. Others however, were grateful for the chance to talk about their perceptions of the abuse.

As the numbers began to reach an acceptable level we decided to form a control group for purposes of comparison. Since most of the men involved in this study were blue-collar workers, we obtained some blue-collar control data by asking forty-five members of a local union (and their wives) to fill out the same questionnaires.

■What We Found

Finally, the day of reckoning: The data were in the computer, carefully lifted from the questionnaire pages, read into the computer file, reread, checked, and double-checked for accuracy. At last we were ready see the results. The initial data runs started. Would the suspected connection of borderline personality to cyclical abusiveness appear as we had hypothesized? It was not unlike the reentry of a jury foreman after a lengthy deliberation. The verdict was imminent.

The first scores we looked at were for Oldham's borderline personality self-report measure. On the face of it, the abusive men, especially those who had referred themselves to treatment, scored very much like diagnosed borderlines. The first hurdle had been crossed. We interpreted the self-referred batterers scores as indicative of a "pure" group of assaultive males.

The court-referred men, on the other hand, were more of a mixed bag, and their scores were lower. Since the criminal justice system works in occasionally capricious ways, this group would have to include a diverse sample of men: those who were repeatedly violent, those who had had one loud altercation that the neighbors overheard and reported to the police, and career criminals who were dumped on the treatment group out of court desperation. It was reasonable that the psychological profile of this group was varied.[19]

We also found strong correlations between borderline scores and the associated features of cyclical abusiveness. Those strongly related to borderline scores included anger, jealousy, and tendencies to blame women for negative events in the relationship. These were certainly consistent with the clinical descriptions of borderlines. What's more, these scores intercorrelated to form a syndrome or personality constellation. I call this constellation the abusive personality.

The jealousy, which the men experienced in the extreme, seemed to me to be a fear of abandonment: they would be left for another who was more sexually desirable. The high borderline men also reported more abuse toward their partners, both physical and emotional. Indeed, borderline personality was strongly related to a constellation of abuse features: anger, blame, and jealousy; telling a woman she was unattractive and undesirable; controlling her use of space and time; or hitting her. Also, the higher the borderline score the greater the problems with alcohol. We wondered if these men drank to blot out the bad feelings that welled up inside them.

The borderline scores were also highly associated with angry or ambivalent attachment—so highly associated, in fact, that we can consider ambivalent attachment and the borderline personality to be almost synonymous.

As we investigated further, some other interesting patterns came to light. One was that the borderline scores were highly related to trauma symptoms. These men suffered more frequently from every aspect of trauma symptoms: depression, anxiety, sleep disturbance, and dissociation. This finding reinforced a common early origin of borderline personality that we described above: childhood abuse, shaming, and weak attachments.

■Why Our Results Make Sense

The shaming father, the ambivalent attachment with the mother, the violence in the home all come together to contribute to the creation of the violence-prone borderline man. Why does he get so angry and abusive in intimate relationships? The answer may lie, in part, in what intimacy means to him.

The borderline man asks his intimate relationships to do the impossible. They serve the unenviable task of gluing together, with relational chewing gum and piano wire, a shaky ego. This flimsy arrangement—and with it, the man's very sense of integrity, his sense of himself as whole—threatens to fail at any time.

Yet the relationship that the man needs so desperately is fraught with "dysphoric stalemates"—abandonment anxiety, extreme demandingness, and an incapacity to communicate intimacy needs. As the tension and malaise build, the borderline man unconsciously requires his wife to take it away, to soothe him, to make him feel whole and good. He has trouble sleeping, he's depressed. But he does not express this because he is either unaware of it or doesn't want to reveal his weaknesses.

Instead, he begins to act out, erupting in hurtful words and actions that distance her. He ruminates on her faults. He yells at her, snapping over little things. He wants to push her away, but sometimes he wants her to save him. The fleeting feeling passes so quickly, he hardly notices it. He's back to hating her. She's such a bitch. If only he could get free of her, he would finally be happy. He starts to drink more heavily. The alcohol seems to dull the unhappiness, but he becomes less restrained, more aggressive. Sometimes it scares him, this energy from within. He feels that it might overwhelm him.

When, as it must, the relationship fails to deliver, or appears in his eyes to fail, his extreme anger results. Then his very sense of self is threatened. Since he uses projection as a defense, he believes this collapse is the woman's fault. He views her, at that phase of the relationship, as all bad.

The man denies or rationalizes as appropriate (given the difficulty in living with his unreasonable spouse) all of these features of his personality. In some cases, of course, the woman *has* become unreasonable, either by virtue of her own personality or by having lived with him too long.

PART III

Is a Cure Possible?

10 Helping the Abusive Man

PEGGY CALLED ME IN A FRENZY. "YOU HAVE TO HELP KEN! HE really needs you!" She went on to describe his tirades, his jealousy, his abusive tantrums, his promises to reform. "This time," she said emphatically, "he means it. He really, really wants to stop."

"Fine," I replied, "tell him to call me."

She wavered. "Well, you see," she stammered, "he wanted me to set it up. He's not sure yet about coming."

This urgency at the peak of crisis, followed by the quick retreat, is what I call "the backoff." The crisis, of course, comes when the woman is about to leave or has left because the assaultive man has gone too far. He wants to get her back, but the thought of therapy is terrifying.

The enormous ambivalence that abusive men bring to treatment is generated by three terrors: There's the fear of being alone—without the woman they've abused for years. Then there's the dread of disclosing their problems in front of strangers, especially male strangers. Worst, however, is the foreboding that something will come up they won't be able to handle, the threat of their own buried fears or shame.

The men's fitful dance is accompanied by the woman's own. In almost every case there has been abuse before. She might have left before. She is staying away this time, but for how long? Maybe she'll come back if he commits to treatment. The tango of traumatic bonding takes over. Both partners are more hooked to the relationship than they want to admit. The woman looks for any miraculous signs that the violence will cease. The man hopes that he can wait her out—that her outrage will pass, that they can go on as if nothing has happened.

Before I admit any man to a therapeutic group, I conduct an extensive interview. One morning, I assessed three men whom the courts had sent to me. The first was a Transylvanian Evangelical who complained that this wife had ruined him by selling the family deli and giving all the proceeds to Jimmy Swaggart. The second was a bond salesman. The interview went well until I asked him if he'd ever been in therapy before. Suddenly, he unleashed a torrent of vitriol against psychologists, whom he claimed were "the cause of those scum walking around downtown." As it turned out, he was heavily involved in a religious cult that fostered a group hatred of psychiatry and psychology. The third was an Italian man who complained that his wife had the anger problem and that the courts had conspired to put him before me. He was not to blame.

I accepted two of these referred men into the group, but I passed on the psychologist-hater. With court-mandated treatment, clients often appear therapy-proof. When I think back to the men whose cases we have described in this book, only Lenny, Meyer, and Colin seemed treatable at first, and Lenny and Meyer, of course, were conning us.

■ Opening Night

What a group session opening night is for those men who finally make the decision and for those whose decision has been mandated by the courts. It's a session filled with tension and potential volatility. On one opening night, a man named Winston became enraged when we suggested he might have a problem with anger. He was huge—built like a football linebacker—and very agitated from the moment he walked in the door. His three marriages had ended in divorce, and he had a record of three prior charges of wife assault. In order to show us we were wrong about his anger problem, Winston began to challenge my cotherapist Jim Browning.

"What are your credentials?" he demanded. "Are you trying to psychoanalyze me? What makes you think you know me better than I do?" Then he stormed out, nearly knocking off our chairs those of us who were between him and the door.

On another occasion Eddie, a cab driver, had a different reaction. Eddie was irascible and vocal. He announced on opening night that he had already been in a treatment group run by another community organization, and it had done nothing for him. Eddie attributed that failure to the therapists and to the minimal effort the men in treatment had exerted. By way of example, he turned to a tiny man seated beside him who spoke with a heavy eastern European accent.

"This guy was telling me, as we waited downstairs, that he was just here to coast through and humor the court." Eddie was yelling now. "That's exactly the kind of bullshit I mean!"

The smaller man jumped out of his seat. "I think I take the other group—the one on Tuesday," he announced as he fled, hat and coat trailing behind him.

Obviously, with a collection of men who convert so much anxiety to anger, there are bound to be fireworks on opening night. However, that's not always the case. One man broke into tears at what his violence had done to his wife's trust. He was inconsolable. The other men were visibly shaken. This was their worst nightmare: one of these touchy-feely, weepy groups.

As I approached the building for one opening night, I saw several men smoking and walking in tight circles. Only one seemed relaxed. That was Lenny. He had already figured out how he would beat the group: what to say, how much to say, how to get into the good graces of the therapists. It was second nature to him. He saw the group as a hurdle to be jumped, nothing more.

Meyer was only somewhat less confident. He had conned the cops, after all. What could these therapists know? He figured that if he told them about what a monster his mother was, he would have them. Therapists were suckers for that kind of thing. Then he could weave in the stuff about Carol's hang-ups, sort of get them on his side.

Robert, on the other hand, didn't look so good. He had the appearance of someone who had just gazed in a mirror and encountered his own inner demons. He sported a frozen semi-smile: the bottom half his face was grinning, the upper half, terrified; the eyes too wide for laughter, the mouth too curved for terror. He knew he couldn't tell the others what he had seen; they would think he was crazy. But there they were, nonetheless. What if those hellhounds he kept locked away came out? A brief flash of panic seared him like a hot coal. He winced at the thought and looked around furtively to make sure no one had noticed. Then he turned his gaze to the pavement.

Colin stood aloof from the rest, carefully smoking a cigarette and flicking lint from his jacket.

Juan Carlos was also standing off by himself, staring at the ground as though he were expecting it to open and a genie to emerge and tell him he didn't have to go through with the therapy, that he was really all right. In fact, better than all right, he was exceptional. Sandra was the loser.

Once inside, the tension was palpable. We seated the men in a circle, facing each other, rendering cover and avoidance all but impossible. Robert and Juan Carlos continued inspecting the floor. Colin looked amiable, if somewhat reserved. He smiled a lot, maybe too much. Lenny was chipper, though, introducing himself to everybody, even shaking hands.

My cotherapist and I gave it about ten extra minutes on opening night, then we started. To the clients, those minutes seemed an eternity. The sizing up had already begun. They were think-ing, "Am I really like these guys?" and wondering how to get through with minimal flack. Soon they would jockey for the position of alpha male. Part of this power struggle would involve challenging us, the therapists.

We began with a brief statement explaining that the group was intended to curb anger, violence, and abuse in intimate relation-ships, that we would be meeting for sixteen weeks, that we understood the men were tense. We started slowly, asking each man to introduce himself by telling us his first name and describ-ing what he had done that led to his participation. The men went in whatever order they wanted. This told us immediately who was shy and who was forthcoming.

The stories on first go-around were typically short and self-serving. Most were presented with much rationalization and self-justification. Men usually specify in great detail what their women did to anger them, accompanied by only traces of how they had incited the conflict or acted violently. The usual excuses about alcohol and financial stress are offered up.

They also display the depth of their denial. "It wasn't that seri-ous," they may say. "Any man would have done the same thing. I'm no worse than my friends." Or, "Other men are more violent and getting away with it." Some claim their religion expects them to be firm. It's commonplace in their culture. Or they blame it all on the lawyer. A few admit to having "a temper." Some come right out and ask for help. Occasionally, men have burst into tears of remorse, making the others even more uncomfortable.

We challenge very little on this first round. Being too con-frontational right away is counterproductive. It raises the shame level and the consequent defensiveness. We just wanted the men to speak, to reduce the tension in the room. I think of the thera-pists in these groups as being like high-wire walkers. You can fall over the side of being too challenging (and generating shame and defensiveness) or the side of not challenging enough (and not confronting past attitudes and beliefs). You learn with experience what works for each man and each group.

Lenny started. "Oh, I hit Sylvia all right, but she asked for it because she wouldn't quit blowing coke. And I caught her in bed with my best friend." He elaborated on his girlfriend's drug and sexual habits, eliciting much sympathy from the group. "You know," he continued, "I pleaded with her to go straight, but none of that matters now. She's out of my life and I'm here to improve myself. I want my next relationship to be the one that goes the distance." His words gushed like water from a broken main.

I asked Lenny how he felt about hitting Sylvia. "I'm glad she's gone. She was bad news." No remorse here.

"What do you want to learn from the treatment group?"

"Just how to manage my anger better and how to get along with people." Then, Lenny broke into some street philosophy. "We're all in this together," he mused. "Life's too short for all the hassles. We've just got to learn to live together."

I was waiting for "And tomorrow is the first day of the rest of my life," but at least he spared me that.

Meyer was next. "Yes, I hit my wife," he admitted. "I feel sorry for that, and I want to do whatever it takes to become nonviolent. Carla and I are still together, and I want to make it work." His speech was calm, even articulate compared to Lenny's. "Marriage is a learning experience," he continued thoughtfully. "How to get along with another person is life's greatest lesson. The arguments are a two-way street, but I realize now that violence is no solution. I just get too angry sometimes, I don't know why."

Robert had been rocking back and forth in his chair and alternately clenching and unclenching his fists. He had to be coaxed to speak.

"Are you nervous?" I asked.

He nodded, "A little."

He talked only about his "red out." He still couldn't remember the attack. It scared him, though. "I was out of control," he said.

"The violence happened too fast. I want help with my bad temper. Next time I could kill somebody, and I want help before that happens."

Colin looked around the room to make sure no one else wanted to speak. Seeing that the podium was clear, he cleared his throat. "You know," he said, "I feel somewhat out of place here because I haven't been violent. I'm not like the rest of you guys. But I'm prepared to learn. There had been one minor incident, but that could have happened to anybody. I lost my cool once and backhanded her."

We asked him to demonstrate a "backhand." He made a motion like a tennis stroke. I suspected that there were other dimensions in which he felt he was dissimilar from the rest—perhaps character and social class.

Juan Carlos took his turn. "The whole thing was a big mistake," he said. "There was no violence. My girlfriend lied because she was angry, and the police ran with it because I didn't show them any respect. They're probably racist. I wouldn't play their game so they busted me. My lawyer told me to plead guilty and just get it over with. A first offense is no big deal, anyway. I'm in the group only because I have to be. Look," he said pointedly, completely oblivious to the contradiction and denial in his statement, "I never did it, and I'll never do it again."

■The Confessions

Underlying the tension on opening night is the fear that one's shameful acts will be exposed. For men who have experienced shaming as boys, this is too much to take right away. Therapists Bob Wallace and Anna Nosko have described the "co-confessional" aspect of opening nights in wife abuse groups.[1] The requirement to attend group and to reveal past transgressions are, themselves, shame-inducing. The exercise of having each client tell his story allows men to overcome their shame through what Wallace and

Nosko call "vicarious detoxification." The listeners encounter their own shame as each member of the group confesses.

Also, projection occurs. By hearing the others confess, the men encounter parts of themselves that they had previously split off. They are stunned to discover someone else describing acts they have tried to deny to themselves. This sets the stage for the therapeutic working through of shame issues. Also, the requirement that each man confess and the group pressure to do so builds solidarity so that eventually anger, rage, and violence, the original defenses against shame, are no longer necessary.

Of course, it would be misleading to say that all this happens on opening night. Only the first steps are taken toward disclosure and group process. We're happy just to get the men to speak, to hear each other, and to air their reactions to each others' stories.

■The Ground Rules

We do one other thing on opening night. We go over the group rules: being on time for meetings, remaining drug- and alcohol-free, keeping what was said in group confidential, maintaining openness and honesty, taking responsibility for one's own violence. In fact, the two biggest obstacles in any group are getting the men to acknowledge the violence and to be accountable for it. If these hurdles aren't cleared, nothing else has any effect.

This concept of personal responsibility for one's actions, which is new to some of the men, is a central theme throughout treatment. Therapeutic groups hold men to a much higher standard of responsibility than does the criminal justice system. We don't accept alcohol as an excuse for violence, and we challenge the men who try to use it. "Why is it that not everyone who gets drunk gets violent?" we ask. "What anger are you carrying around? How do you express that anger? Do you have to get drunk to express it? Why?"

Some men have strong reactions to signing a group contract that explicitly states they will take personal responsibility for their violence. Some get angry and stalk out, only to return remorsefully the following week. Others try a variety of defenses such as denial and wife-blaming. The trick for us as therapists is to develop a group momentum toward accepting personal responsibility. The path toward that goal has been paved with broken marriages, injured wives, frightened children, and even the man's own health.

This educational aspect is accompanied by modeling of taking responsibility. We usually try to include in our group men from past groups who have already arrived at this attitude. When Eddie, who was so angry on opening night, discovered that the group was helping him, he wanted to give something back. We kept him on as a facilitator for the next group. His natural confrontational skills simply needed some softening and refining. Having a few self-referred men in the group helps, too. They, by definition, admit to having a problem.

We consider ourselves in good shape if half the men confess openly on the first night. The momentum usually shifts in the direction of openness for most of the men by the third week. The rest may or may not be reachable. We have learned that each man has a personal pace based on past trust, the degree of shame, and his capacity for honesty.

We also explain confrontation on opening night. It is designed to help the men by giving them a different and challenging perspective on themselves—a perspective they would not otherwise receive. Confrontation is not meant as an attack, nor as an effort to tear the men down, but to make them stronger, better, more in control of themselves. "Nobody will be put down here," we tell them, "but you can expect to be confronted."

■ Weeks Two Through Five

Week two begins with another lesson. We teach the basics: how to separate conflict issues from feelings and actions. We ask, "What do you fight about?" These are the conflict issues. Since they are usually similar for many men (money, sex, in-laws, child-rearing), this brings the group together some more.

We explain that feelings are one's internal reactions to conflict. We ask, "Can you understand the meaning of fear, humiliation, shame, or grief? What would you feel if you weren't angry in this situation?" This also serves to explain the basis of anger as a feeling that overrides fear or other emotions. Finally, we explore all the possible actions that one can take during conflict. It's a wide range and the men see a broader spectrum of options than when they started.

They learn to recognize points at which they could stop, compromise, and de-escalate the anger. They realize that their power needs and a desire to win drive their choices to escalate the conflict. We try to get them to stop seeing marital conflicts in win-lose terms, but as a situation in which both parties win if the conflict is successfully resolved.

We define physical, sexual, and verbal abuse of people, property, or pets. We explain that abuse is designed to hurt the other. We detail why this sets up a perpetual chain of recriminations. Referring to a list of specific abusive actions, we ask the men, "Did you ever do this?" Then, "What else in this category have you done? Has this ever been done to you?"

These learning aspects impart information, but they also reach the men personally and help define the group. The participants begin to relate to the content of arguments that other men have with their wives. "Oh yeah," they say, "that happens to you, too?"

This can be another tightrope issue for therapists. Some group cohesiveness is good, especially if it facilitates disclosure, but we cannot let it turn into bonding based on anti-female feelings. We do this by pointing out the men's similarities on the issues and stresses of their lives and then challenging any negative generalizations about women.

We must confront wife-blaming, too, but if we come down on a man too soon for condemning his partner, he'll decide that we're unsympathetic and clam up. Timing is everything. We establish rapport first, then start the confrontation. This is best undertaken once the man begins to recognize his pattern of blaming his spouse as a means to avoid his own responsibility for violence.

Week three starts with what is by now familiar. We ask, "Was there any abuse last week? If so, what happened? How did you feel about what you did? How could you have handled it differently? Did you take time out and talk yourself down? How did you do that? How did you feel about it after?"

The approach is still nonconfrontational, merely examining the problem. To ensure that the men feel this is their issue and not something we are forcing on them, we do another exercise developed by psychologist Jim Browning. At the end of the previous session, we had asked every man to think about his personal "violence policy." Now he has the opportunity to report it.

In his violence policy, the man must enumerate those situations in which he feels it is acceptable for him to use violence. Typically, most men describe self-defense or protection of family members. (I've never encountered anyone in treatment who said that wife assault was generally acceptable.) The man makes his personal standard public and explicit. It's important that this policy statement come from him. In that way, he feels it's his own objective; his own energy initiates it. A therapist lecturing, dictating, or ordering a man to be nonviolent boomerangs with many men.

We hold the men to that policy in the weeks to come, but we do not simply accept any policy as given. The exercise provides an opportunity to discuss the effects of violence in producing retribution and anger in the victim. It becomes an exercise in applied philosophy.

Usually during that third session, we distribute our research questionnaires. Often the men react with hostility to our probing into the past since their childhood experiences trigger a sense of shame. Sometimes it takes four or five reminders before the men return the surveys.

By week four, we instruct the men on how to chart and monitor their anger, using an anger diary. This deceptively simple device teaches them to dissect an anger episode into the trigger (what was said or done to initiate the anger), an anger rating (how extreme the anger was on a personal ten-point scale), how they recognized the anger (what physical reactions occurred), the "talk up" (what thoughts the man had as he was becoming increasingly angry—the so-called bitch tape), and finally the "talk down" (how he soothed himself and lowered his anger level).

This exercise gives us a lens into the man's inner thought processes. Since the rules require him to report the trigger as objectively as possible, while the talk up is pure interpretation, he reveals the biases, distortions, anxieties, and assumptions that construct his anger. This, then, becomes the shared substance of group process and is examined and corrected through group feedback.

For example, after Robert shared the talk up preceding his rage over Carol's lateness from school, the issue went to the group. "How many of you would feel like Robert?" we asked. Those who expressed that they would or would not were drawn out. The men started to notice commonalities in inner experience, feelings that had not been shared before.

By this stage, the group is beginning to solidify; men exchange phone numbers, set up crisis lines for each other, and develop friendships that persist outside the group. At week five, we decide who to cut loose. If a participant is dismissing the work, refusing to take responsibility for his violence, or is still in denial, we therapists and the group turn up the heat and confront him. Sometimes the confrontation goes along the lines of, "I'm doing the work and you're just goofing off." Eddie would often initiate these exchanges.

The emotional intensity of every group hits its peak when we finally open up the issue of early experience with one's parents. We usually ask the men to describe in an open-ended way what their family was like, but we also probe with specific questions about how parents expressed anger.

We split the group into sections to cover more intimately these difficult early experiences. We relate their feelings about having been victimized by their parents to events in their current families. We ask, "Do you want to break the generational cycle?"

Two of the four men in my group one evening had been abused by their mothers and had had their hands around their mothers' throats in retaliation. Both let go. Jack's mother forced him to beat up and jump on his baby brother's head. If he didn't do it, she whipped him with a leather strap. He came into the group as an unemployed, twenty-three-year-old father of three kids. He had never resolved the fury he experienced from the beatings in his youth and was bewildered and overwhelmed by his current difficulties.

The biggest conscious rage-inducer from mothers, though, seemed to be not physical abuse but the boy's knowledge that his mother had a lover. The men who disclosed this seemed to be the most furious. Sam told the group how his mother had had sex with her boyfriend while his father was in the hospital recovering from a heart attack. His rage was palpable as he described it.

These disclosures cement the group. Typically the men have never talked to anyone about their victimization. They tried to do the "manly thing" and deal with it silently. The primitive emotionality is sometimes shattering. In one group, a man recounted an incident that had occurred eight years earlier. He had never shared this with anyone.

He was driving a long distance with his wife when he fell asleep at the wheel. The car crashed, and she was killed. He stumbled from the wreck, and when it was apparent she was dead, he called her father to tell him the horrible news. His words: "You know your daughter? Well, she's dead, you know?" No voice, no words of grief or commiseration, no emotional vocabulary at all beyond the most rudimentary. In his limited way, he expressed remorse about this in the group.

The End of the Group

As the weeks pass, two or three marriages break up; a child is born; some men lose their jobs; some run afoul of the law. In one group, members informed us, Kenny won't be here tonight: We saw him on the six o'clock news, getting arrested for a botched bank heist.

And all along, we teach the difference between confrontation and attack, point out defensiveness, raise consciousness, steer the group through didactic and process stages, interview the wives, pour the coffee, and turn out the lights.

We educate the men on how to recognize and express emotions. We teach them breathing and stretching exercises to release tension. We model assertiveness and negotiation skills as a means of heading off serious conflict. We explore other ways of feeling a sense of power in their lives—power that doesn't require the domination of another. What this may be varies from man to man. For some, it's as simple as getting out into nature. For others, it's engaging in a meaningful hobby.

It's clear that the men have abused those around them. But we also raise the issue of how they have abused themselves. We remind them about how much suffering they experience and the extent to which they blot it out with alcohol or drug binges.

Some men do well. Others can never recover from early deficits in the ability to recognize emotions—a skill they should have mastered as children, but that is so hard to learn now that they are grown.

At the end of the treatment program, the main issue for men who were afraid of coming to the group, is how to replace the intimacy and camaraderie they have found there. The dismal prospect of going back to superficial conversations in sports bars doesn't please them. Some maintain group-initiated friendships for years; others drift back to isolation.

■The Spiraling Path to Change

Men who are sent by the courts to treatment for wife assault are addicted to violence. They use it as a release from anger and depression, a way to take control and resolve conflicts, and a tension reducer. They know of no alternatives when they enter treatment. Often, they can't even acknowledge their role or take the problem seriously.

Psychologist James Prochaska studied people with a variety of addictions such as alcohol, cocaine, and tobacco and found that the path from addiction to freedom is rarely linear.[2] Rather it's a spiral process made up of six stages characterized by advances and back-sliding. Most clients take a step backward now and then. Preparation for this is called "relapse prevention." This model can also be applied to the assaultive man.

In the first, or *precomtemplation* stage, the batterer hasn't quite accepted that he has a problem, although others may be bringing it to his attention. Certainly, the arrest and conviction for wife assault should be a red flag, but the man may not be convinced yet that it's *his* problem. This is another reason court-mandated treatment is so important for the violent man. It cuts through the ambivalence and gives him a clear requirement to attend a group—not that he's happy about it. There are still huge hurdles to overcome.

The *contemplation* stage involves acknowledging that there is a problem. *Preparation* encompasses seeking help; *action* means taking the cure. *Maintenance* requires one to stay "sober" or violence-free, and *termination* means that the changed self has reconstituted—constant watchfulness and maintenance are no longer needed.

This is not an easy path, however. Hardly anyone gets from precontemplation to termination on the first try. For each two steps up the spiral there may be one step back. Violent men often relapse, especially if they're trying to come from the earliest stages in the recovery spiral. In the process, however, the man must learn not to let the relapse undercut his motivation to change, but to keep moving toward termination of the addiction no matter what. And a woman partnered with someone going through treatment must recognize that an initial short-term treatment group will not be a magic bullet to stop the violence once and for all. Often, it's a good first step.

The road to change must include alternative ways of tension reduction and the learning of negotiation skills and a commitment to the process of compromise.

■ Do the Groups Reduce Domestic Violence?

Given the prior damage and constellation of current problems that most men bring to treatment, it seems that any reduction in repeat violence is a miracle. I have found, however, that treatment does accelerate change, so that eventually the time from first arrest to last known violence shortens and the number of repeat offenses diminishes.

For men with borderline personalities, more thorough treatment (longer than sixteen weeks) is probably required. But for those with psychopathic personalities, such as vagal reactors (those who become internally calmer and more focused while they batter their wives), treatment may be unproductive. This group is an enormous burden for society because it includes the chronic repeat offenders—serial batterers, who create a disproportionate amount of violence. We tracked one man, for example, who had been charged with twelve wife assaults in ten years. He had never been incarcerated for very long.

We either have to generate the political will to keep these repeat assaulters in locked facilities or to mark these men in some way that would warn innocent potential victims. I have sometimes facetiously suggested that we apply an indelible warning signal to some part of the man's anatomy to at least give a woman an early sign of his lethal potential. Of course, civil libertarians would scream. But I say, if you repeatedly beat up women, you lose some liberties.

In 1986, I did a follow-up study in which we contacted thirty-seven women partners of men who had completed treatment.[3] Eighty-four percent reported no serious violence after treatment.

I also compared fifty men who had completed treatment with fifty matched untreated controls who had also been arrested for wife assault. The untreated men refrained from violence so long as their probation was in effect. According to the police, only 4 percent reoffended. But when their probation expired, they returned to form, with arrests for repeat assaults against their wives, the recidivism rate, jumping to 40 percent within two and a half years of the original conviction. The treated group, on the other hand, maintained the 4 percent recidivism rate throughout the same period.

Faye Resnick reports how the suppressive effect of external sanctions was borne out in the Simpson case: "O. J. had been charged with battering Nicole after police found her cowering outside her house in 1989, badly beaten and dressed only in a bra and sweat pants. O. J. did not want a repeat of even the minor media stories published about that incident."[4] Resnick interprets the resulting two-year probation as responsible for Simpson displaying good behavior from 1989 to 1992. This included sparing a man whom he had observed having sex with Nicole during one of his stalkings, according to Resnick. External sanctions can suppress physical abuse so long as the man feels himself to be under surveillance (such as on probation).

Others have found that if the man completes treatment, his chances of reoffending drop substantially.[5] Police records indicate recidivism rates of 8 percent for treated men and 24 percent for untreated controls.

We recently completed a much larger, ten-year follow-up of six hundred treated and two hundred untreated men.[6] The two groups were alike in all respects except that the treated group had completed sixteen weeks of therapy, whereas the untreated had been recommended for therapy but for practical or logistic reasons could not attend or had dropped out early. We used Canadian Police Information Centre data to determine recidivism. Any police record on subsequent charges for wife assault anywhere in the country would show up there.

We traced men as far back as ten years. The treated men had only a slight (3 percent) edge in success with no repeat arrests. But as we looked further at the groups that continued to assault, we found the untreated men and dropouts were less successful at remaining violence-free. This group had a larger proportion of repeat offenders, and the men were arrested twice as often as those who completed treatment. For every 1,000 treated men, there were 350 fewer arrests in ten years. However, that was just part of the story.

Criminologists have known for years that arrests are just the tip of the iceberg for most crimes. For every assault reported, there are several more committed. For example, in our interviews with the partners of men in our study, we found that for each arrest, there had been 30 attacks. In other words, for every group of 1,000 assaultive men who complete treatment, 10,500 fewer attacks would be committed in a ten-year period than if the men had not been treated.

Although my findings indicate the necessity and efficacy of treatment, we still have to be cautious in our interpretation. There might have been some factor in the men themselves that differed between the groups—such as their motivation to change. Men who complete the group are the most motivated, so exposure to treatment and motivation are directly related. We cannot attribute outcomes of treatment to either cause alone. Nevertheless, no psychological treatment works for someone who has no motivation. No forced remedy has a lasting therapeutic effect, including brainwashing, electroshock, and castration.[7]

Moreover, it's hard to imagine that the untreated men were a psychologically more difficult group that those who were treated. Steve Hart, Teresa Newlove, and I found personality disorders in about 85 percent of men referred for wife assault treatment.[8] Hardly an easy group to change, given their deep-seated problems and initial wariness toward psychotherapy. Our study again showed that two types of personality disorder make the man a worse bet for treatment: the antisocial or vagal reactors described in Chapter 2, and the borderline personality.

I'm unaware of any attempt to evaluate the effects of individual treatment on becoming nonviolent. My hunch is that individual treatment is frequently not mandated and the man doesn't have the social support to get him through the first sixteen weeks. As a consequence, the dropout rate is high, and often men leave treatment prematurely.

I've often been asked about the efficacy of couples treatment. It's certainly a viable form of treatment, too. However, it's advisable that a thorough assessment of the man be made to ensure that his violence has stopped before couples therapy is undertaken. Otherwise, the woman can be put at risk by the therapeutic process itself.

The results of my research clearly shows, however, that violence is reduced by group therapy by 10,500 attacks per 1,000 men over ten years. However, one reason for caution is that men with extreme personalities (especially antisocial or severe borderline disorder) would be least likely to benefit from such treatment.

■ Of Despair and Hope

After sixteen years of doing this work, I still find myself being surprised. I have learned to be humbled in my power of prediction. There are men who I thought would never be able to stop beating their wives, but they have, for reasons that only partially have to do with therapy. Perhaps their transformation is dependent on a desire to make a change in their lives—a change that one would call magical. Every group has in it at least one man who seems hopeless, but who improves dramatically. That's what keeps me coming back for more.

According to their wives, Eddie and Colin remained violence-free after treatment. Eddie, as I explained, joined another group of his own volition. Meyer's wife left him. There was no more physical violence, but he continued to be so emotionally abusive after treatment that she wanted out. Theirs was a messy divorce with lawyers and recriminations. The last I heard, they were still battling over money. She was sure he had squirreled away tons of it in Swiss bank accounts. But there are no further assault charges against him. He has either straightened out or left the country.

Lenny has reoffended.

Robert, surprisingly, has not. Two years after his group was over, he came to see me. He disclosed that he was now in individual therapy. He was dealing with his adoption and searching for his birth parents. Carol had left him over the incident with the key; she never got over it. But he was now in a new, nonviolent relationship.

Even therapists get fooled in their predictions of future violence. Juan Carlos assaulted another woman but came back to the group a changed man. He admitted he was in denial the first time through and began to work seriously on himself. He became violence-free and became a counselor to street kids.

Sometimes I wonder how I'm going to be able to help certain clients. Frank was a truck driver. He had been in a relationship with his wife for twelve years and had beaten her weekly during that time. They had three kids. I had to work with my own prejudices. He had no education. I wasn't sure he would be able to understand the therapeutic exercises. But he wanted to change. He kept plugging away at it. He quit drinking and faithfully showed up to group. Two and a half years later, there was still no violence.

The men who have the greatest success try to make holistic life changes. They must ask themselves, "What's my place in this world? What's important to me? Who am I, after all?" All we therapists can do in sixteen weeks is open the possibility for change. Therapy is a lifelong process for these men.

Some of them find their way to ongoing support groups such as twelve-step programs. There are even long-term support groups for abusers in which therapists conduct more in-depth work with smaller groups. Some of the men who go through this process later train to become facilitators. The program at a federal prison near Vancouver is currently run by one of these former abusers.

Borderlines travel through life with damaged egos. It's as if they're driving a car that has a leaky tire. Every few miles, they must stop to inflate it. If they're constantly thinking about inflating their ego, how do they have time to consider other humans, with their needs and desires?

I often have a sense of the immense neediness and loneliness that these men experience. Many live and die without ever knowing who they really are. They sit around the campfire of life, staring into the dark, and only the eyes of a beast glare back from beyond the light. Despite the male trappings of power, they experience profound powerlessness. They are alienated from themselves. They don't understand why the rages overtake them; they're out of touch with the shame that precipitates the violence; they are unable to grieve or mourn the absence of love in their lives—the absence of what they wanted from their parents but couldn't get.

In group, we just scratch the surface of these issues. Sometimes I feel as if I'm staring at an ocean of despair and can't fathom the bottom.

These men live in a culture of sports and escapism and alcohol. In group, we have taught them anger management and communication skills, but behind that is the exposure to human contact. For many, the group is the first time in their lives that they've had an emotionally honest relationship with another human and been able to talk about their vulnerabilities and feelings. They finally learn to trust another. The friendships the men form in group last for years. The interaction generates contact that never existed before. It is my hope that this bond will have some effect on the men, even if the results of therapy aren't immediately apparent.

If you take away the violence, what is left? Emptiness? Robotic civility? Can these men ever learn to love—to seriously comprehend and accept another person and care about her at least as much as they care about themselves? I don't know the answer to that question. But my deepest and most fervent hope is that they can.

⬛11 Some Practical Tips

As you read this book, if you are a man you may have identified yourself in the descriptions, or if you're a woman you may have finally found an explanation and an understanding of your partner's puzzling and dangerous behavior. After the shock of recognition, the question remains, what to do about it, how to deal with it.

⬛ For Women

When you understand and acknowledge the danger signs of abusiveness, you may spare yourself and your partner years of pain and grief. If someone with whom you are involved is accurately portrayed in this book, it would be helpful for you to analyze the extent of his violence potential. The following are risk factors for danger in intimate relationships:

- Your partner's description of his parents'—especially his father's—rejecting or shaming behavior.

- Your partner's or other family members' recollections of physical assault directed at him or at his mother.

- Your partner's personality indicators such as frequent anger and jealousy or an intense fear of abandonment.

- Your partner's trauma symptoms, such as constant sleep disturbances and nightmares, memory losses for specific events, panic attacks, crying, and depression.

- Your partner's alcohol or drug abuse to numb himself to his internal pain.

- Your partner's blaming orientation. Does he hold you responsible for his actions or feelings? Does he insist that everything is always your fault?

- Your partner's cyclical mood swings that seem to have nothing to do with you but incorporate a theme of your being all good or all bad—a Madonna or a whore.

If you believe your partner has some of these risk factors, ask yourself the following questions:

- Does he seem like two people, showing one face to his friends and the public and another to you in private?

- Does he go through a cycle of buildup, explosion, and contrition?

- Has he been violent with you? Once? Twice? Have these been isolated events tied to a particular triggering situation, or does his abusiveness seem to occur for no apparent reason?

- Is his physical attack accompanied by verbal assaults, such as calling you a bitch, cunt, whore, or slut?

- Have there been circumstances (such as separations or jealousies) that might have triggered the violence? How did he act? Did he behave like the men in this book?

- Have you ever missed work from the effects of abuse?

- Have you ever used makeup or dark glasses to hide bruises, or have you covered up by making excuses to a doctor or coworker for injuries sustained during an attack?

If your partner has been violent repeatedly or if his violence seems to be related to his personality—that is, accompanied by jealousy, blaming, and cyclical flareups—he will need help to stop. Although national surveys show that about one-third of abusive men resist further attacks spontaneously, many of these men have hit their wives only once. Their violence is not personality-driven, and does not occur repeatedly or stem from within.

But if the abusiveness has already occurred repeatedly, and if it takes more than one form—emotional as well as physical—it probably will not cease without outside intervention.

The first step in seeking that intervention is to ensure your own safety:

- Call the police if you feel physically threatened.

- Find or create a safe place in your home where you can barricade yourself in and which has access to a phone.

- Carry a cellular phone for emergencies.

- Create a support network of friends and family to whom you can turn regardless of the hour or day.

It's important to tell your partner when you feel afraid. But when you do, ascertain if he can hear you. Does he acknowledge his anger not only when in a contrition phase but when *you* want to talk about it? Under no circumstances should you accept the blame for his being angry or abusive. These are his feelings and actions. If he cannot accept ownership of them, he will never change them.

Also bear in mind that personality-based abusiveness serves many purposes for the abuser:

- It makes him feel powerful.

- It forges his shaky identity.

- It enables him to control you and "win" arguments with you.

Your partner is not likely to relinquish this habit easily.

Talking about their abusiveness generates shame in many men. And that, in turn, raises the anger level. *Do not try to be your partner's therapist.* Address your own fears of him. Make "I" statements such as "I get afraid (or irritated) when you raise your voice," rather than "you" statements such as "You're always shouting at me." Insist that he seek and obtain therapeutic help. If he backslides, let him know it. If he persists in backsliding, you should seriously consider leaving.

If you leave, you will need to have a plan of action. An important step is having a group of supportive women to whom you can talk about your concerns and who can add an element of security to your life. It's best to live with other women for at least four months—one year is even better. This is a maximum risk period for stalking and continued or escalating violence, and you will need support and safety. If you feel harassed or believe you are being stalked, a restraining order can help.

Remember, you know your partner better than anyone else. Abusive men have idiosyncratic patterns of action. Some respond to a woman's threat to leave by seeking help. Others become more unstable and belligerent. You will have to make these determinations in planning your strategy. If you are going to leave, make sure you are safe before you announce your intention to your partner. And make note of his reaction for future reference. Some men never relinquish their abusiveness, others change dramatically, and most relapse on the way to change.

Could you handle a relapse? Has your partner already promised to change repeatedly and relapsed just as often? If so, why are you staying?

I offer these questions only as guides to analyzing your own situation. The decision to stay or leave is yours alone. It is a difficult one. If this book has helped you better understand the basis of your partner's abusiveness, you can make a more informed decision.

■For Men

If you have recognized your own behavior and feelings in this book, you may have previously experienced a gnawing awareness that you have a problem. If you have not already entered some form of psychotherapy, I would urge you to *begin immediately*.

I am not an alarmist. The truth is, you have nothing to lose and much to gain by entering a treatment group for anger and assaultiveness. You could derive self-control and self knowledge, an end to a painful cycle of tension and abuse, enhanced relationships with women, and a release from the constant sense of internal despair. You can control your anger rather than be controlled by it. You will also have an opportunity to encounter other men at a deeper level and forge friendships you never believed possible.

There are certain kinds of groups to stay away from, however. For example, I would avoid certain "men's movement" groups that encourage the expression of anger toward women. These are likely to polarize men and women all the more; they may help you find additional justifications for the anger that you have directed at your partner. Rather than teaching you to to express that anger more effectively or understanding its source within you, these groups will favor your externalizing it and acting it out, using group-sanctioned rationalizations to continue to find fault with your partner. Not all "men's movement" groups are like this; however, it is important to be aware of what you are getting into.

It's also possible to find yourself in a group that is at the opposite end of the spectrum, a group for so-called "feminist men." Again, I say, beware. Such groups can organize around a shame of maleness that can undermine your ability to understand your feelings. Indeed, many "unacceptable" or "politically incorrect" feelings such as anger with your partner are suppressed or ignored in groups such as these.

Both extremes are psychologically unhealthy for a man who is trying to understand and control his anger. In general, the less ideology the group has, the better. Stay away from gurus or any situation that feels politically extreme. If you feel you are stifling your thoughts and feelings in the group, try expressing them. Do you feel safe in doing so? Do you feel listened to and understood? Do you accept that sometimes you will be challenged and confronted in the group? Is this done in a constructive way?

It's best to phone around. Talk to your local United Way chapter. This organization usually has a family services group that focuses on anger management. Ask what other groups are available locally and ask what is involved in treatment. Beware of simplistic generalizations about men—all men are not alike. Churches, synagogues, mosques, court services, and civic mental health programs all can point you toward available treatment.

In general, group treatement is favored over individual therapy. The support that develops in groups serves to maintain attendance. It's too easy to drop out prematurely from individual therapy.

Also be aware that it is natural to experience some anxiety and a sense of shame at seeking treatment. Do not let it deter you. In four months you will have learned a lot about yourself. Only your anxiety and shame can stand in the way of this giant step toward a better intimate relationship.

Notes

■ Chapter 1. Drowning in a Red Tide

1. "Ballet Master Held on Charge He Beat His Wife." *New York Times*, July 22, 1992. Note that the July 23, 1992, *Times* reported that the charges had been dropped.
2. *New York Times*, June 26, 1994.
3. D. G. Dutton and B. Levens (1977).
4. R. E. Worden and A. Pollitz (1984).
5. E. Fromm (1973), pp. 322–323.
6. F. Resnick and M. Walker (1994), pp. 9, 39.
7. M. Crawford and R. Gartner (1992), p. 44. The authors drew from police records and coroners' reports to examine 551 recorded femicides in the Province of Ontario from 1974 to 1990.
8. S. Coren and K. B. Mah (1993), also K. Strachan and D. G. Dutton (1992).
9. More than 70 percent, according to M. A. Straus, R. J. Gelles, and S. Steinmetz, 1980.
10. E. Stark, A. Flitcraft, and W. Frazier (1979). Some dispute exists, however, over a category the authors labeled as "probable" victims of wife assault. The evidence for this category was flimsy. A smaller category was based on sounder evidence.
11. R. J. Gelles and M. A. Straus (1992).
12. Straus, Gelles, and Steinmetz (1980), p. 3.
13. Ibid., p. 34.
14. Testimony, p. 10,823; see Crawford and Gartner (1992), also M. Daly and M. Wilson (1993).

15. Crawford and Gartner (1992).
16. Testimony, p. 10,825; G. M. Wilt and R. K. Breedlove (1977).

■Chapter 2. Are All Batterers Alike?

1. Straus and Gelles, pp. 95–127.
2. Resnick and Walker, p. 115.
3. D. G. Saunders (1992), p. 269. Saunders's "Type 3" men, whom he calls "emotionally volatile," fit descriptions of the abusive personality. They are more angry, depressed, jealous, and "emotionally volatile" than other abusive males. They made up 31 of 165 in Saunders's sample, although some men in other "types" (clusters) may have qualified as well if they had been assessed for abusive personality.
4. Straus, Gelles, and Steinmetz (1980).
5. S. D. Hart, D. G. Dutton, and T. Newlove (1993), p. 334. Meeting criteria for antisocial behavior in a court-referred group were 45 percent, 37.5 percent in a self-referred group. Saunders (1992) found "Type 2" (generally violent) men in a wife assault sample to be 48 of 165 (29 percent).
6. R. D. Hare (1993), p. 34.
7. Ibid., p. 170.
8. See D. Olwens, J. Block, and M. Radke-Yarrow (1986).
9. Saunders (1992). The men who were most severely abused are the most abusive toward their wives.
10. N. Jacobson (1993), p. 6. See also J. M. Gottman et al. (1995).
11. N. Jacobson. Personal communication, 1994.
12. Jacobson (1993), p. 6.
13. Saunders (1992) reported that 86 of 165 wife assaulters fit his "Type 1" profile of overcontrolled.
14. R. Tolman (1989). *The Psychological Maltreatment of Women Inventory* developed by Richard Tolman in 1989 has fifty-eight items or statements that the woman checks as happening to her on a 1 (never) to 5 (very frequent) basis. The item by item scores yield two "factors" or sets of mathematically interrelated items. These reveal two prominent abuse themes: dominance/isolation and emotional abuse. The higher the score, the more frequently the male partner used the behaviors listed under that factor.
15. D. G. Dutton and J. J. Browning (1988), pp. 168–172.

■Chapter 3. The Cycle of Violence and the Abusive Personality

1. L. E. Walker (1979).
2. Resnick and Walker (1994), p. 9.

3. Ibid., p. 10.
4. Dutton and Browning (1988), pp. 166–174.
5. D. G. Dutton and S. Yamini (1995), pp. 45–48.
6. See D. G. Dutton, B. Fehr, and H. McEwen (1982), pp. 14–16.
7. R. Baumeister (1990), pp. 99–101.
8. Dutton and Yamini (1995), pp. 39–48.
9. M. Rosenbaum (1990), pp. 1036–1039.
10. D. G. Dutton and A. Starzomski (1992), pp. 203–222.
11. "A Tale of Abuse," *Newsweek,* December 12, 1988, p. 56.
12. See D. G. Dutton and S. Painter (1981, 1993a, 1993b).
13. A. Freud (1942).
14. B. Bettelheim (1943).
15. Dutton and Painter (1981, 1993a, 1993b).

■ Chapter 4. Post-Traumatic Stress Disorder: A Telling Clue

1. F. Elliott (1977), p. 98.
2. Ibid., p. 104.
3. B. Egeland (1993). Egeland found that 40 percent of adults who maltreat their children were themselves abused as children.
4. Elliott (1977), p. 105.
5. A. Rosenbaum and S. Hoge (1989), p. 1048.
6. A. R. Felthous and S. Bryant (1991), p. 73.
7. See E. O. Wilson (1977).
8. D. Buss (1994), p. 158.
9. Ibid., p. 157.
10. R. J. Gelles (1975).
11. T. Davidson (1978).
12. Gratian's *Decretum* cited in ibid., p. 99.
13. Ibid.
14. D. G. Dutton (1988), p. 10.
15. Davidson (1978), p. 113.
16. R. E. Dobash and R. P. Dobash (1979), p. 24
17. V. Goldner, P. Penn, M. Sheinberg, and G. Walker (1990), p. 345.
18. M. Bograd (1988), p. 17.
19. See D. G. Dutton (1995a), pp. 7–11.
20. D. H. Coleman and M. A. Straus (1986), p. 148.
21. G. Lie et al. (1991).
22. D. G. Dutton and M. A. Landolt (1995).
23. D. Romero, "Target: Parents," *Los Angeles Times*, March 21, 1995, sec. E.
24. A. Bandura (1979).
25. Ibid.

26. D. S. Kalmuss (1984), pp. 11–19.
27. D. G. Dutton (1995b).
28. B. van der Kolk (1987).
29. C. Perris et al. (1980).
30. Dutton (1995b).

▪Chapter 5. Shame: The Father's Contribution

1. M. E. Seligman (1975), pp. 40–52.
2. See, for example, D. G. Dutton (1994); D. G. Dutton, A. Starzomski, and L. Ryan (1994); D. G. Dutton, A. Starzomski, and C. van Ginkel (in press).
3. Gelles, in M. A. Straus and R. J. Gelles (1992), pp. 279–286.
4. L. Terr (1990), p. 113.
5. J. Katz (1991), pp. 24–27.
6. L. Sheingold (1989), p. 24.
7. E. Fromm (1963), pp. 35–41.
8. P. Mones (1991), pp. 47–81.
9. See Dutton and Painter (1981, 1993a, 1993b).
10. L. Jackson (1991), pp. 14–15, 17, 233.
11. See S. Weller (1995), p. 59.
12. T. Carpenter (1994), pp. 84–100.
13. J. Tangney et al. (1992). For earlier work, see also H. B. Lewis (1971).
14. L. Wurmser (1981).
15. Katz (1991), p. 22.
16. Ibid., p. 24.
17. Ibid., p. 29.
18. van der Kolk (1987), pp. 40–49.

▪Chapter 6. Ambivalent and Angry Attachment: The Mother's Contribution

1. H. F. Harlow and M. K. Harlow (1971).
2. Ibid., p. 206.
3. M. Klein and J. Riviere (1937).
4. M. Mahler, F. Pine, and A. Bergman (1975).
5. Ibid., p. 77.
6. Ibid., p. 95.
7. Ibid., p. 96.
8. Ibid., p. 101.
9. Klein and Riviere (1937), p. 38.
10. Ibid., p. 39.

11. Klein and Riviere (1937), pp. 8–10; based on a lecture given in 1936.
12. K. Adam (1994); D. Brent et al. (1993); Dutton and Yamini (1995).
13. Resnick and Walker, p. 153.
14. Ibid., p. 170.
15. Ibid., p. 172.
16. D. Winter (1973), p. 171.
17. Bettelheim (1943).
18. Bowlby (1977), p. 203.
19. Bowlby, cited in R. Karen (1994).
20. Ibid., p. 169.
21. Bowlby (1969, 1973, 1980).
22. Bowlby (1973), p. 284.
23. Bowlby (1977), p. 203.
24. Bowlby (1980), p. 11.
25. Bowlby (1973), pp. 289–290.
26. M. D. S. Ainsworth et al. (1978).
27. R. Karen (1990), p. 50.
28. M. Main and D. R. Weston (1982).
29. Karen (1990), p. 50.
30. L. E. Walker (1984).
31. D. G. Dutton, K. Saunders, A. Starzomski, and K. Bartholomew (1994).
32. Dutton (1995b).

■Chapter 7. Learning the Ways of Violence

1. For example, M. Miedzian (1991).
2. Straus et al. (1980) and D. S. Kalmuss (1984). The same increased likelihood of being both a victim and a perpetrator of intimate violence also existed for women.
3. D. G. Dutton and S. D. Hart (1992b); Egeland (1993).
4. Egeland (1993), p. 203.
5. R. Novaco (1976), p. 1124.
6. Fromm (1973), p. 322.
7. G. R. Patterson, R. A. Littman, and W. Brickner (1967).
8. Winter (1973), p. 172.

■Chapter 8. The Assaultive Man as an Adolescent

1. L. Marshall and P. Rose (1990).
2. C. Turner, M. Fenn, and A. Cole (1981).
3. E. H. Erikson (1963).
4. M. Schumacher (1995).

5. A. Starzomski and D. G. Dutton (1993).
6. Dutton, Saunders, Starzomski, and Bartholomew (1994).

■Chapter 9. The Borderline Male: The Cycle of Fear and Rage

1. J. G. Gunderson (1984).
2. O. Kernberg (1977), p. 118.
3. L. E. Walker (1979), pp. 55–70.
4. T. Millon (1981).
5. Ibid., p. 333.
6. Ibid., p. 348.
7. Ibid.
8. Ibid., pp. 349–350.
9. Millon (1991).
10. See van der Kolk (1987); M. C. Zanarini et al. (1989).
11. E. H. Carmen, P. P. Rieker, and I. E. Mills (1984).
12. D. G. Dutton and S. D. Hart (1992a) and C. Widom (1989) for a discussion of both the early onset and long-term effects of borderline personality organization and child abuse.
13. J. Oldham et al. (1985).
14. Ibid., p. 14.
15. Ibid.
16. J. Briere and M. Runtz (1989).
17. Doing this resulted in my being turned down on a research grant application. The reviewer said it wasn't ethical for the men to feel any coercion to participate, but didn't offer any alternative method for getting data from reluctant perpetrator populations.
18. See D. G. Dutton and K. J. Hemphill (1992) and D. G. Dutton and A. Starzomski (1994) for a discussion of these processes in abusive men.
19. See Dutton and Starzomski (1994) for an extended discussion of these differences.

■Chapter 10. Helping the Abusive Man

1. R. Wallace and A. Nosko (1993), p. 45.
2. J. O. Prochaska et al. (1992), p. 1104.
3. D. G. Dutton (1986).
4. Resnick and Walker, pp. 47–48.
5. See B. D. Rosenfeld (1992).
6. D. G. Dutton, M. Bodnarchuk et al. (1995).
7. See Schein (1961) for brainwashing; see also N. Heim (1981).
8. Hart, Dutton, and Newlove (1993).

References

Adam, K. (1994). Suicidal behavior and attachment. In M. B. Sperling & W. H. Berman (eds.), *Attachment in adults* (pp. 275–298). New York: Guilford.

Ainsworth, M. D. S., Blehar, M. C., Waters, E., & Wall, S. (1978). *Patterns of attachment: A psychological study of the strange situation.* Hillsdale, NJ: Erlbaum.

"Ballet Master Held on Charges He Beat His Wife." *New York Times,* July 22, 1992.

Bandura, A. (1979). The social learning perspective: Mechanisms of aggression. In H. Toch (ed.), *Psychology of crime and criminal justice* (pp. 298–336). New York: Holt, Rinehart & Winston.

Baumeister, R. (1990). Suicide as an escape from the self. *Psychological Review, 97* (1), 90–113.

Bettelheim, B. (1943). Individual and mass behavior in extreme situations. *Journal of Abnormal and Social Psychology, 38,* 417–432.

Bograd, M. (1988). Feminist perspectives on wife abuse: An introduction. In M. Bograd & K. Yllo (eds.), *Feminist perspectives on wife abuse* (pp. 11–26). Beverly Hills: Sage.

Bowlby, J. (1969). Attachment and loss. Vol. 1, *Attachment.* New York: Basic Books.

Bowlby, J. (1973). Attachment and loss. Vol. 2, *Separation.* New York: Basic Books.

Bowlby, J. (1977). The making and breaking of affectional bonds. *British Journal of Psychiatry, 130,* 201–210.

Bowlby, J. (1980). Attachment and loss. Vol. 3, *Loss, sadness, and depression.* New York: Basic Books.

Briere, J., & Runtz, M. (1989). The trauma symptom checklist (TSC-33): Early data on a new scale. *Journal of Interpersonal Violence, 4* (2), 151–162.

Brent, D., et al. (1993). Personality disorder, tendency to impulsive violence and suicidal behavior in adolescents. *Journal of the American Academy of Child and Adolescent Psychiatry, 32* (1), 69–75.

Buss, D. (1994). *The evolution of desire: Strategies of human mating.* New York: Basic Books.

Carmen, E. H., Rieker, P. P., & Mills, I. E. (1984). Victims of violence and psychiatric illness. *American Journal of Psychiatry, 141,* 378–379.

Carpenter, T. (1994, November). The man behind the mask. *Esquire, 122* (5), 84–100.

Coleman, D. H., & Straus, M. A. (1986). Marital power, conflict, and violence. *Violence and Victims, 1* (2), 141–157.

Coren, S., & Mah, K. B. (1993). Prediction of physiological arousability: A validation of the Arousal Predisposition Scale. *Behavior Research and Therapy, 31* (2), 215–219.

Crawford, M., & Gartner, R. (1992). *Woman killing: Intimate femicide in Ontario, 1974–1990* (p. 44). Womens Directorate, Ministry of Social Services, Toronto, Ontario.

Daly, M., & Wilson, M. (1993). Spousal homicide risk and estrangement. *Violence and Victims, 8* (1), 3–16.

Davidson, T. (1978). *Conjugal crime: Understanding and changing the wife beating pattern.* New York: Hawthorn.

Dobash, R. E., & Dobash, R. P. (1979). *Violence against wives: A case against the patriarchy.* New York: Free Press.

Dutton, D. G. (1986). Wife assaulters explanations for assault: The neutralization of self-punishment. *Canadian Journal of Behavioral Science, 18,* 381–390.

Dutton, D. G. (1988). *The domestic assault on women: Psychological and criminal justice perspectives.* Boston: Allyn & Bacon.

Dutton, D. G. (1994). The origin and structure of the abusive personality. *Journal of Personality Disorders, 8* (3), 181–191.

Dutton, D. G. (1995a). *The domestic assault of women.* Vancouver: University of British Columbia Press.

Dutton, D. G. (1995b). Trauma symptoms and PTSD profiles in perpetrators of abuse. *Journal of Traumatic Stress, 8* (2), 299–315.

Dutton, D. G., Bodnarchuk, M., Kropp, R., Hart, S., & Ogloff, J. (1995). *A tenyear follow-up of treated and untreated wife assaulters.* Manuscript submitted for publication, B.C. Institute on Family Violence, Vancouver, B.C.

Dutton, D. G., & Browning, J. J. (1988). Concern for power, fear and intimacy, and aversive stimuli for wife assault. In G. T. Hotaling, D. Finkelhor, J. T. Kirkpatrick, & M. A. Straus (eds.), *Family abuse and its consequences: New directions in research* (pp. 163–175). Newbury Park, CA: Sage.

Dutton, D. G., Fehr, B., & McEwen, H. (1982). Severe wife battering as deindividuated violence. *Victimology: An International Journal, 7* (1–4), 13–23.

Dutton, D. G., & Hart, S. D. (1992a). Risk markers for family violence in a federally incarcerated population. *International Journal of Law and Psychiatry, 15,* 101–102.

Dutton, D. G., & Hart, S. D. (1992b). Evidence for long-term specific effects of childhood abuse and neglect on criminal behavior in men. *International Journal of Offender Therapy and Comparative Criminology, 36* (2), 129–138.

Dutton, D. G., & Hemphill, K. J. (1992). Patterns of socially desirable responding among perpetrators and victims of wife assault. *Violence and Victims, 7* (1), 29–39.

Dutton, D. G., & Landolt, M. A. (1995). *Personality correlates of abusiveness in gay and heterosexual males.* Unpublished manuscript, Department of Psychology, University of British Columbia.

Dutton, D. G., & Levens, B. (1977). Domestic crisis intervention: attitude survey of trained and untrained police officers. *Canadian Police College Journal, 1* (2), 75–90.

Dutton, D. G., & Painter, S. (1981). Traumatic bonding: The development of emotional attachments in battered women and other relationships of intermittent abuse. *Journal of Victimology, 6,* 139–155.

Dutton, D. G., & Painter, S. (1993a). Emotional attachments in abusive relationships: A test of traumatic bonding theory. *Violence and Victims, 8* (2), 105–120.

Dutton, D. G., & Painter, S. (1993b). The battered woman syndrome: Effects of severity and intermittency of abuse. *American Journal of Orthopsychiatry, 63* (4), 614–622.

Dutton, D. G., Saunders, K., Starzomski, A., & Bartholomew, K. (1994). Intimacy-anger and insecure attachment as precursors of abuse in intimate relationships. *Journal of Applied Social Psychology, 24* (15), 1367–1386.

Dutton, D. G., & Starzomski, A. (1992). *Personality precursors of alcohol use and wife assault.* Unpublished manuscript, Department of Psychology, University of British Columbia.

Dutton, D. G., & Starzomski, A. (1994). Psychological differences in court-referred and self-referred wife assaulters. *Criminal Justice and Behavior, 21* (2), 203–222.

Dutton, D. G., Starzomski, A., & Ryan, L. (1994). *Antecedents of Borderline Personality Organization in wife assaulters.* Manuscript submitted for publication, University of British Columbia.

Dutton, D. G., Starzomski, A., & van Ginkel, C. (in press). The role of shame and guilt in the intergenerational transmission of abusiveness. *Violence and Victims.*

Dutton, D. G., & Yamini, S. (1995). Adolescent parricide: An integration of social-cognitive theory and clinical views of projective-introjective cycling. *American Journal of Orthopsychiatry, 65* (1), 39–48.

Egeland, B. (1993). A history of abuse is a risk factor for abusing the next generation. In R. J. Gelles & D. R. Loseke (eds.) *Current controversies on family violence.* Newbury Park, CA: Sage.

Elliott, F. (1977). The neurology of explosive rage: The episodic dyscontrol syndrome. In M. Roy (ed.), *Battered women: A psychosociological study of domestic violence.* New York: Van Nostrand.

Erikson, E. H. (1963). *Chilhood and society.* 2nd ed. New York: Norton.

Felthous, A. R., & Bryant, S. (1991). The diagnosis of intermittent explosive disorders in violent men. *Bulletin of the American Academy of Psychiatry and Law, 19* (1), 71–79.

Freud, A. (1942). *The ego and the mechanisms of defense.* New York: International Universities Press.

Fromm, E. (1973). *The anatomy of human destructiveness.* New York: Fawcett.

Fromm, E. (1963). *The art of loving.* New York: Bantam.

Gelles, R. J. (1975). Violence and pregnancy: A note on the extent of the problem and needed services. *The Family Co-ordinator, 24,* 81–86.

Gelles, R. J., & Straus, M. A. (1992). The medical and psychological costs of family violence. In M. A. Straus & R. A. Gelles (eds.), *Physical violence in American families.* New Brunswick, NJ: Transaction Publishers.

Goldner, V., Penn, P., Sheinberg, M., & Walker, G. (1990). Love and violence: Gender paradoxes in volatile attachments. *Family Process, 29,* 343–364.

Gottman, J. M., Jacobson, N. S., Rushe, R. H., Short, J. W., Babcock, J., La Taillade, J. J., & Waltz, J. (1995). The relationship between heart rate activity, emotionally aggressive behavior and general violence in batterers. *Journal of Family Psychology, 9,* 1–41.

Gunderson, J. G. (1984). *Borderline personality disorder.* Washington, DC: American Psychiatric Press.

Hare, R. D. (1993). *Without conscience: The disturbing world of the psychopaths among us.* New York: Pocket Books.

Harlow, H. F., & Harlow, M. (1971). Psychopathology in monkeys. In H. D. Kinnel (ed.), *Experimental psychopathology.* New York: Academic Press.

Hart, S. D., Dutton, D. G., & Newlove, T. (1993). The prevalence of personality disorder amongst wife assaulters. *Journal of Personality Disorders, 7* (4), 329–341.

Heim, N. (1981). Sexual behavior of castrated sex offenders. *Archives of Sexual Behavior 10* (1), 11–19.

Jackson, L. (1991). *LaToya: Growing Up in the Jackson Family.* New York: Dutton.

Jacobson, N. (1993, October). *Domestic violence: What are the marriages like?* American Association for Marriage and Family Therapy, Anaheim, CA.

Kalmuss, D. S. (1984). The intergenerational transmission of marital aggression. *Journal of Marriage and the Family, 46,* 11–19.

Karen, R. (1990, February). Becoming attached. *Atlantic Monthly,* 35–70.

Karen, R. (1994). *Becoming attached.* New York: Warner Books.

Katz, J. (1991). *Seductions of crime.* New York: Basic Books.

Kernberg, O. (1977). The structural diagnosis of borderline personality organization. In P. Hartocollis (ed.), *Borderline personality disorders: The concept, the syndrome, the patient* (pp. 87–121). New York: International Universities Press.

Klein, M., & Riviere, J. (1937). *Love, hate and reparation.* New York: W. W. Norton.

Lie, G., Schilit, R., Bush, J., Montague, M., & Reyes, L. (1991). Lesbians in currently aggressive relationships: How frequently do they report aggressive past relationships. *Violence and Victims, 6* (2), 121–135.

Mahler, M., Pine, F., & Bergman, A. (1975). *The psychological birth of the human infant.* New York: Basic Books.

Main, M., & Weston, D. R. (1982). Avoidance of the attachment figure in infancy: Descriptions and interpretations. In C. M. Parks & J. Stevenson-Hinds (eds.), *The place of attachment in human behavior.* London: Tavistock.

Marshall, L., & Rose, P. (1990). Premarital violence: the impact of family of origin violence, stress, and reciprocity. *Violence and Victims, 5*, 52–64.

Miedzian, M. (1991). *Boys will be boys.* New York: Doubleday.

Millon, T. (1981). *Disorders of personality, DSM III, Axis II.* New York: Wiley.

Millon, T. (1987). On the genesis and prevalence of the borderline personality disorder: A social learning thesis. *Journal of Personality Disorders, 1* (4), 354–372.

Mones, P. (1991). *When a child kills: Abused children who kill their parents.* New York: Simon & Schuster.

Novaco, R. (1976, October). The functions and regulations of the arousal and anger. *American Journal of Psychiatry, 133* (1), 1124–1128.

Oldham, J., Clarkin, J., Appelbaum, A., Carr, A., Kernberg, P., Lotterman, A., & Haas, G. (1985). A self report instrument for Borderline Personality Organization. In T. H. McGlashan (ed.), *The borderline: Current empirical research. The progress in psychiatry series* (pp. 1–18). Washington, DC: American Psychiatric Press.

Olwens, D., Block, J., & Radke-Yarrow, M. (eds.). (1986). Development of antisocial behavior and delinquency. *Clinical Psychology Review, 10*, 1–41.

Patterson, G. R., Littman, R. A., & Brickner, W. (1967). Assertive behavior in children: A step toward a theory of aggression. *Monographs of the Society for Research in Child Development, 32* (5), serial no. 133.

Perris, C., Jacobsson, L., Lindstrom, H., von Knorring, L., & Perris, H. (1980). Development of a new inventory for assessing memories of parental rearing behavior. *Acta Psychiatrica Scandinavica, 61*, 265–274.

Prochaska, J. O., DiClemente, C. C., & Norcross, C. C. (1992). In search of how people change: Applications to addictive behaviors. *American Psychologist, 47* (9), 1102–1114.

Resnick, F., & Walker, M. (1994). *Nicole Brown Simpson: The private diary of a life interrupted.* New York: Dove.

Romero, D. (1995, March 21). Target: Parents. *Los Angeles Times*, section E.

Rosenbaum, A., & Hoge, S. (1989). Head injury and marital aggression. *American Journal of Psychiatry, 146* (8), 1048–1051.

Rosenbaum, M. (1990). The role of depression in couples involved in murder-suicide and homicide. *American Journal of Psychiatry, 147* (8), 1036–1039.

Rosenfeld, B. D. (1992). Court-ordered treatment of spouse abuse. *Clinical Psychology Review, 12,* 205–226.

Saunders, D. G. (1992). A typology of men who batter: Three types derived from cluster analysis. *American Orthopsychiatry, 62* (2), 264–275.

Schein, E. H. (1961). *Coercive persuasion: A socio-psychological analysis of the brainwashing of American civilian prisoners by the Chinese communists.* New York: Norton.

Schumacher, M. (1995). *Crossroads: The life and music of Eric Clapton.* New York: Hyperion.

Seligman, M. E. (1975). *On depression, development and death.* San Francisco: Freeman.

Sheingold, L. (1989). *Soul murder: The effects of childhood abuse and deprivation.* Fawcett: New York.

Stark, E., Flitcraft, A., & Frazier, W. (1979). Medicine and patriarchal violence: The social construction of a private event. *International Journal of Health Services, 9* (3), 461–493.

Starzomski, A., & Dutton, D. G. (1993). *Attachment style and emotional reactions to intimate conflict.* Manuscript submitted for publication. University of British Columbia.

Strachan, K. & Dutton, D. G. (1992). The role of power and gender in anger responses to jealousy. *Journal of Applied Social Psychology, 22* (22), 1721–1740.

Straus, M. A., & Gelles, R. J. (1992). *Physical violence in American families.* New Brunswick, NJ: Transaction Publishing.

Straus, M. A., Gelles, R. J., & Steinmetz, S. (1980). *Behind closed doors: Violence in the American family.* Garden City, NY: Anchor/Doubleday.

"A Tale of Abuse." *Newsweek,* December 12, 1988, pp. 56–65.

Tangney, J., Wagner, P., Fletcher, C., & Gramzow, R. (1992). Shamed into anger? The relation of shame and guilt to anger and self reported aggression. *Journal of Personality Disorders, 62* (4), 669–675.

Terr, L. (1990). *Too scared to cry: Psychic trauma in childhood.* New York: Harper & Row.

Terr, L. (1991). Childhood traumas: An outline and overview. *American Journal of Psychiatry, 148* (1), 10–20.

Tolman, R. (1989). The development of a measure of psychological maltreatment of women by their male partners. *Violence and Victims, 4* (3), 159–177.

Turner, C., Fenn, M., & Cole, A. (1981). Social psychological analysis of violent behavior. In R. B. Stuart (ed.), *Violent behavior: Social learning approaches.* New York: Brunner/Mazel.

van der Kolk, B. (1987). *Psychological trauma.* Washington, DC: American Psychiatric Press.

Walker, L. E. (1979). *The battered woman.* New York: Harper & Row.

Walker, L. E. (1984). *The battered woman syndrome.* New York: Springer.

Wallace, R., & Nosko, A. (1993). Working with shame in group treatment of male batterers. *International Group Psychotherapy, 43* (1), 45–61.

Weller, S. (1995). *Raging heart*. New York: Simon & Schuster.

Widom, C. (1989). Does violence beget violence? A critical examination of the literature. *Psychological Bulletin, 106*, 13–28.

Wilson, E. O. (1977). *On human nature*. Cambridge: Harvard University Press.

Wilt, G. M., & Breedlove, R. K. (1977). *Domestic violence and the police: Studies in Detroit and Kansas City*. Washington, DC: Police Foundation.

Winter, D. (1973). *The Power motive*. New York: Free Press.

Worden, R. E., & Pollitz, A. (1984). Police arrests in domestic disturbances: A further look. *Law & Society Review, 18* (1), 105–119.

Wurmser, L. (1981). *The mask of shame*. Baltimore: Johns Hopkins University Press.

Zanarini, M. C., Gunderson, J. G., Marino, M. F., Schwartz, E. O., & Frankenburg, F. R. (1989). Childhood experiences of borderline patients. *Comprehensive Psychiatry, 30* (1), 18–25.

Zimbardo, P. (1969). *The human choice: Individuation, reason and order vs. deindividuation, impulse and chaos*. Nebraska Symposium on Motivation, University of Nebraska Press.

Index

Abandonment fantasies, 14–17, 34; attachment and, 107–14; in borderline personality, 145–46, 149, 154; of cyclical/emotionally volatile batterers, 34–35; of infant, 98–99, 103; language and, 16, 66; origins of, 98–99; rage and, 16–17; sexual themes in, 14–16, 138–39; shame and, 88–89; sociobiological explanation for, 66–67; triggering events for, 24, 43, 45–46, 111

Abuse excuse, 82

Abuse victims: batterers as, 19–20, 74–77, 84–90, 170–71; blaming the victim syndrome and, 44, 46, 49, 146, 167, 168–69, 183; denial patterns of, 13–14, 55; fuzzy memories of, 89; learned helplessness of, 80, 125; post-traumatic stress disorder and, 53; Stockholm syndrome and, 56, 87; traumatic bonding and, 54–57, 160

Abusive personality: attachment patterns in, 76, 95–96, 106, 107, 113–16, 122, 130; borderline characteristics of, 153–54; direct experience of abusiveness and, 76, 117–30; dulling of emotions in, 85–86, 126, 139, 147; measuring tendency toward, 136–37; misogyny in, 138–39; personality disorders and, 176–77; purposes for abuser, 183–84; seeds of, 76, 133–35; shame and, 76, 92–93, 122, 125, 130, 179

Action stage, 173

Acute battering phase, 46–49, 153

Adolescence, 131–39; emergence of abusiveness in, 133–35; individual psychotherapy in, 124; preabusive patterns in, 92–93, 135–39

Agentic behavior, 73, 127, 139

Aggression: abnormal, 61–62; "Bobo doll" research on, 71–72; and brain damage theory of abuse, 61–65; and male privilege, 69–70; normal, 61; and post-traumatic stress disorder, 75; predatory, 128–29; projection of, 105; separation from mother and, 110–11;